# Best Easy Day Hikes
# Seattle

## Help Us Keep This Guide Up to Date

Every effort has been made by the author and editors to make this guide as accurate and useful as possible. However, many things can change after a guide is published—trails are rerouted, regulations change, techniques evolve, facilities come under new management, etc.

We appreciate hearing from you concerning your experiences with this guide and how you feel it could be improved and kept up to date. While we may not be able to respond to all comments and suggestions, we'll take them to heart and we'll also make certain to share them with the author. Please send your comments and suggestions to the following address:

Globe Pequot Press
Reader Response/Editorial Department
246 Goose Lane, Suite 200
Guilford, CT 06437

Thanks for your input, and happy trails!

# Best Easy Day Hikes Series

# Best Easy Day Hikes
# Seattle

Second Edition

## Allen Cox

**FALCON**GUIDES

GUILFORD, CONNECTICUT

# **FALCON**GUIDES®

An imprint of The Rowman & Littlefield Publishing Group, Inc.
4501 Forbes Blvd., Ste. 200
Lanham, MD 20706
www.rowman.com
Falcon and FalconGuides are registered trademarks and Make Adventure Your Story is a trademark of The Rowman & Littlefield Publishing Group, Inc.

Distributed by NATIONAL BOOK NETWORK

Copyright © 2021 The Rowman & Littlefield Publishing Group, Inc.

Maps by Melissa Baker

British Library Cataloguing-in-Publication Information Available

**Library of Congress Cataloging-in-Publication Data Available**

ISBN 978-1-4930-5374-2 (paper)
ISBN 978-1-4930-5375-9 (electronic)

# Contents

## The Hikes

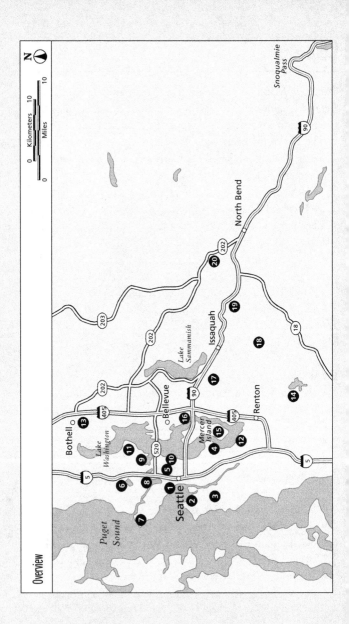

Overview

# Acknowledgments

First, I would like to extend my appreciation to all who advocate for sensible land management and the conservation of public lands and wild habitats. Without their work, few places such as the ones included in this guidebook would be set aside for the rest of us to enjoy.

I would like to thank the land management agencies responsible for the trails included in this guidebook for their cooperation and assistance: Seattle Parks and Recreation, King County Parks, Washington State Parks, Washington State Department of Natural Resources, US Forest Service, and University of Washington.

My sincere appreciation goes out to my editor, Katherine O'Dell, and the outstanding team at Globe Pequot Press for their guidance and clarity in helping me shape this guidebook.

Lastly, I am grateful to Robert Pruett, Roger Ward, and Dana Price, my dear friends and hiking companions who know how to appreciate an easy day hike. Without them, researching this book would have required many lonely hours on the trail.

# Introduction

## The Lay of the Land—and Water

When you fly into Seattle on a clear day, it appears that there's more water than land. It is a city on and of the water. Puget Sound makes up Seattle's entire western border, and the vast Lake Washington, the eastern. A ship canal slices the city in half as it passes through yet another lake, Lake Union, and connects the two larger bodies of water. The Duwamish River snakes through the city's south end and empties into Elliott Bay—Seattle's busy commercial port.

With Seattle water-locked on two sides and land-locked on its narrower north and south ends, the only way to grow is up. Neighboring municipalities sprawl north, south, and across Lake Washington, which is spanned by two floating bridges. With all that water, one of Seattle's greatest attributes is its miles of waterfront property, shoreline public space, and dramatic water views.

East across Lake Washington sits another lake nearly as long, Lake Sammamish, with the neighboring cities of Redmond, Bellevue, and Issaquah lining its shores. Beyond that, continuing east and up, the Cascade foothills rise with plenty of land set aside for public use.

What does this landscape do for recreational opportunities in and around the city? If you guessed boating, sailing, swimming, scuba diving, bicycling, jogging, and even parasailing, you'd be correct. But let's not forget about hiking. Seattleites love to hit the trail and take out-of-towners along on the walk. Networks of trails in and around the city offer a variety of settings and terrains, from urban waterfront hikes with stunning views of Seattle's skyline to quiet treks through old-growth forest. The King County Regional Trail System is one of the nation's largest with 175 miles (and growing) of public, multi-use trails, so there's a hike in the Seattle area to suit every hiking ability.

This second edition of this guidebook eliminates some hikes included in the first edition that are farthest from Seattle and replaces them with more easy day hikes within Seattle. In addition, the order of hikes in the Table of Contents has been rearranged to list the in-city hikes first. All hikes are within a 30-minute drive of downtown Seattle, and none requires a ferry ride across Puget Sound.

## Seattle-Area Boundaries and Corridors

For the purposes of this guide, the best easy day hikes are located throughout the city and stretch into parts of King County.

Interstate 5 is the main north-south artery through Seattle. From Interstate 5, Interstate 90 and S.R. 520 both head east via floating bridges across Lake Washington. Directions to trailheads are given from either downtown Seattle or one of these three main arteries.

## Weather

Seattle enjoys a temperate, generally cool climate with four distinct seasons, few extremes, and an average of 58 days bathed in full sun. The city receives only about 38 inches of annual rainfall over an average 156 days a year. So how did it earn a reputation as one of the wettest US cities when in fact it doesn't even rank among the top ten?

Seattle is tucked between the Olympic and Cascade Ranges where clouds gather from the Pacific and can loom for long stretches. When it rains, the city tends to get misted with protracted periods of drizzle. The rainiest seasons are late fall and winter when torrential Pacific storms occasionally blow through.

There's an old quip about Northwesterners having webbed feet. The truth is that they don't often let a cloudy day or a little drizzle slow them down. Cloudy, wet days in the Pacific Northwest possess their own beauty. The forests glisten and come alive. Fog and mist shroud the hilltops and define contours otherwise not seen. The air is fresh, with grit and dust washed away. With the right gear, you can still enjoy the local trails, rain or shine.

Part of being prepared for your hike is checking the weather forecast. If weather conditions are potentially hazardous, which is rare, postpone your hike. If weather conditions are favorable for a safe experience on the trail, enjoy yourself, rain or shine.

## Wildlife

Wildlife shares the spotlight with Pacific Northwest scenery on trails in and around Seattle. Bald eagles soar over wooded parks and perch in treetops above beaches. Great blue herons strike motionless hunting poses in shoreline shallows. Pileated woodpeckers hammer away at the trunks of decaying trees. Cormorants occupy pilings, their wings spread wide to air-dry after their last dive for a meal.

Birdlife is so abundant in Seattle that bird enthusiast groups conduct annual bird counts in several of Seattle's city parks; trails in some of these parks are included in this guidebook.

You might spot deer, raccoons, coyotes, and even red foxes near wooded trails. Lucky hikers near Puget Sound have been known to spot seals and sea lions and, on rare occasions, orcas.

Of course, it's possible to take a hike in and around Seattle without seeing anything more than a few seagulls. Wildlife doesn't usually stage an entrance just to be noticed by humans. Be on the lookout for the wild inhabitants near the trail, and you might be surprised at which critters are watching you.

Encounters with large wildlife are extremely rare, but not unheard of, especially on trails in the foothills. Some trailheads post information about what to do if you encounter a bear or cougar. An excellent source of information regarding such encounters to read before your hike is "Living with Wildlife" by Washington Department of Fish and Wildlife, found at https://wdfw.wa.gov/species-habitats/living.

## Be Prepared

Hiking in Seattle and the surrounding area is generally safe. Still, you should be prepared, whether you are out for a short urban stroll along Seattle's waterfront or venturing into the more secluded Cascade foothills. The following tips will help you prepare:

- Research trail conditions in advance by checking the appropriate land management agency's website or calling their office.
- Check the weather forecast. If it predicts potentially hazardous weather, postpone your hike.
- Hazards along some trails include uneven footing, steep drop-offs and slippery trail surfaces, such as mud, ice,

and wet boardwalks. Trekking poles and proper footwear with good tread can help you maintain your balance in more challenging areas.

- For the day hikes in this guide, pack this guidebook, water, snacks (depending on the length of the hike), rain gear (if the forecast predicts rain), and a compact first aid kit.

- Prepare for extremes of both heat and cold by dressing in layers.

- Most area trails have cell phone coverage. Bring your device, but make sure you turn it off or put it on the vibrate setting if you are hiking in a place where a cell phone ring might disturb wildlife or fellow hikers.

- Make sure children don't stray from the designated route. Children should carry a whistle; if they become lost, they should stay in one place and blow the whistle to summon help.

- Many of the waterfront hikes in this book are not safe for swimming. Swim at designated swimming beaches only, with a companion and preferably a lifeguard present.

## Zero Impact

Trails in the Seattle area are heavily used year-round. We, as trail users and advocates, must be especially vigilant to make sure our passage leaves no lasting mark. Here are some basic guidelines for preserving trails:

- Pack out all your own trash, including biodegradable items like orange peels, or deposit it in a designated trash container. You might also pack out garbage left by less considerate hikers.

- Don't approach or feed wildlife—the squirrel eyeing your energy bar is best able to survive if it remains self-reliant.

- Don't pick wildflowers or gather rocks or other treasures along the trail. Removing these items will take away from the next hiker's experience.

- Stay on the established route to avoid damaging trailside soils and plants. This is also a good rule for avoiding poison oak and stinging nettle, common regional trailside irritants.

- Don't create shortcuts, which promote erosion and damage native vegetation.

- Be courteous by not making loud noises while hiking.

- Many of these trails are multiuse, which means you'll share them with other hikers, runners, skaters, bicyclists, and equestrians. Familiarize yourself with the proper trail etiquette. As a pedestrian, you generally have the right of way, but you should yield when common sense dictates.

- Use restrooms and outhouses at trailheads or along the trail.

## Land Management

The following government and private organizations manage the public lands described in this guide and can provide more information on these and other trails in their service areas:

- Seattle Parks and Recreation, 100 Dexter Ave. N. Seattle, WA 98109; (206) 684-4075, TTY (206) 233-1509; www.seattle.gov/parks. A complete listing of city parks, information about park facilities, and maps for most parks are available on the website.

- Port of Seattle, P.O. Box 1209, Seattle, WA 98111; (206) 787-3000; www.portseattle.org.
- King County Parks, 201 S. Jackson St., KSC-NR-0700, Seattle, WA 98104; (206) 477-4527; www.kingcounty .gov/recreation/parks.aspx. A complete listing of county parks and information about park facilities and trails is available on the website.
- University of Washington (Washington Park Arboretum), 2300 Arboretum Dr. E., Seattle, WA 98112; (206) 543-8800; www.depts.washington.edu/wpa.
- University of Washington (Botanic Gardens), 3501 N.E. 41st Street, Seattle, WA 98195; (206) 543-8616; https:// botanicgardens.uw.edu.
- Washington State Parks, 1111 Israel Rd. S.W., Tumwater, WA 98501-6512; (360) 902-8844; https://parks.state .wa.us.
- State of Washington Department of Natural Resources, 1111 Washington St. S.E., Olympia, WA 98504; (360) 902-1000; www.dnr.wa.gov.

## Public Transportation

This guidebook includes driving directions to trailheads but does not include information on public transportation routes, schedules, or fares. King County Metro Transit provides transit service to or near most trailheads in this book. Call (206) 553-3000 or visit https://kingcounty.gov/depts/ transportation/metro.aspx.

# How to Use This Book

This guide is designed to be simple and easy to use. Each hike is described with a map and summary information that delivers the trail's vital statistics including length, difficulty, fees and permits, park hours, canine compatibility, and trail contacts. Directions to the trailhead are also provided with trailhead GPS coordinates, along with a general description of what you'll see along the way. A detailed route finder (Miles and Directions) provides mileages between significant landmarks along the trail.

## Hike Selection

This guide describes trails that are accessible to every hiker. The longest hike is a 6-mile loop, and most are considerably shorter. They range in difficulty level from flat excursions perfect for a family outing to more challenging hikes in the Cascade foothills with some elevation gain. These trails were selected to represent a wide diversity of terrain, scenery, and experiences. Keep in mind that nearby trails, often in the same park or preserve, may offer options better suited to your needs and abilities. These hikes are spaced throughout the Seattle area, so wherever your starting point you'll find a great easy day hike nearby.

## Difficulty Ratings

These are all easy hikes, but easy is a relative term. In the Seattle area, hills are a fact of life, but many of the hikes in this guidebook have no elevation gain at all, while others have moderate elevation gain.

To aid in the selection of a hike that suits your particular needs and abilities, each is rated easy, moderate, or more challenging. Bear in mind that even most challenging routes can be made easier by hiking within your limits, being prepared, using trekking poles, and resting when you need to.

- **Easy** hikes are generally short and flat, taking no longer than an hour or two to complete.
- **Moderate** hikes involve increased distance and/or slight changes in elevation or may take longer than one to two hours to complete.
- **More challenging** hikes feature some steep stretches, more elevation gain, greater distances, or may take longer than two hours to complete.

These ratings are subjective. What you consider easy is entirely dependent on your level of fitness and the adequacy of your gear (primarily shoes). If you are hiking with a group, you should select a hike with a rating that's appropriate for the least fit and least prepared hiker in your party.

Approximate hiking times assume that on flat ground, most walkers average 2.5 miles per hour. Adjust that rate by the steepness of the terrain and your level of fitness (subtract time if you're an aerobic animal; add time if you're hiking with kids or are easily distracted by trailside attractions), and you will arrive at an approximate hiking duration. Be sure to add more time if you plan to take part in other activities, such as picnicking, birdwatching, or photography.

# Trail Finder

# Map Legend

|  |  |
|---|---|
| ══⑤══ | Interstate Highway |
| ══⑱══ | State Highway |
| ══ | Local Roads |
| ══════ | 4WD Roads |
| ▬▬▬▬ | Featured Trail |
| - - - - - | Trail |
| +—+—+—+ | Railroad |
| ～～ | River/Creek |
| ‿‿ | Marsh/Swamp |
| ⬭ | Ocean/Lake |
| ▭ | Local Park/Golf Course |
| ▭ | State Park |
| ⚓ | Boat Launch |
| •—• | Gate |
| ‿ | Bridge |
| ⚓ | Lighthouse |
| ⚑ | Observation Tower |
| 🅿 | Parking |
| ▲ | Peak |
| ■ | Point of Interest/Structure |
| 🚻 | Restroom |
| ○ | Town |
| ❶ | Trailhead |
| ⧉ | Viewpoint/Overlook |
| ⋙ | Waterfall |

# 1  Myrtle Edwards Park–Elliott Bay Park

This urban bayside hike near Seattle's busy waterfront follows a flat, paved path past landscaped gardens and world-class sculptural installations. The trail traverses two adjoining shoreline parks, the entire length showcasing spectacular city, bay, mountain, and island views with plenty of opportunities to spot marine wildlife.

**Distance:** 3.4 miles out-and-back.
**Approximate hiking time:** 1.5 hours.
**Difficulty:** Easy, flat trail.
**Trail surface:** Paved.
**Best season:** Year-round.
**Other trail users:** Foot traffic only; a designated bike path runs parallel.
**Canine compatibility:** Leashed dogs permitted.
**Fees and permits:** None required.

**Schedule:** Open daily; Myrtle Edwards Park is open 24 hours a day; Elliott Bay Park is open 6:00 a.m.–11:00 p.m.
**Maps:** Any Seattle street map, or USGS Seattle South R, WA and Seattle North R, WA.
**Trail contacts:** Seattle Parks and Recreation (for Myrtle Edwards Park): (206) 684-4075, www .seattle.gov/parks; Port of Seattle (for Elliott Bay Park): (206) 728-3654, www.portseattle.org/community/resources/parks/index.shtml

**Finding the trailhead:** The trail is accessible from the north or south end. The south trailhead is located on the waterfront at the foot of Broad Street and is the best access point for those who are downtown on foot. Hikers wanting free parking should begin the hike at the north trailhead at the opposite end of the park. To access the north trailhead from downtown, drive north on Elliott Ave., turn left on W. Galer St., and turn left after one short block. The street ends at the park's parking lot. The south trailhead GPS coordinates are: N47 36.91' / W122 21.31'.

## The Hike

The Myrtle Edwards Park–Elliott Bay Park Trail was designed to showcase the best of Seattle's scenery—downtown skyscrapers, the iconic Space Needle, Puget Sound, Seattle's busy port, Bainbridge Island, the Olympic Mountains, and Mt. Rainier—and it does not disappoint.

The south trailhead begins at the fountain between Pier 70 and Seattle Art Museum's Olympic Sculpture Park. If you have an extra half-hour to spare, touring this free-admission outdoor sculpture park is a great way to either begin or end your hike.

The shoreline trail through these narrow parks is paved and flat and parallels a bicycle path among acres of grassy hillocks, landscaped gardens, picnic tables, benches, and sculptural installations.

Approximately midpoint up the trail, you will pass a sign that welcomes you to Elliott Bay Park, but not to worry—you're not lost. Elliott Bay Park, managed by the Port of Seattle, is a seamless extension of Myrtle Edwards Park, which is managed by Seattle Parks and Recreation and named in honor of Myrtle Edwards, a former member of the Seattle City Council who championed the conservation of much of the city's land as public space.

Continuing north, you will come to a formal rose garden surrounded by a boxwood hedge. Beside the garden, an outdoor exercise station is waiting for anyone compelled to add some push-ups, pull-ups, or crunches to their hike. Beyond the rose garden, you will pass Port of Seattle's Pier 86 Grain Terminal, and then Elliott Bay Fishing Pier where you can

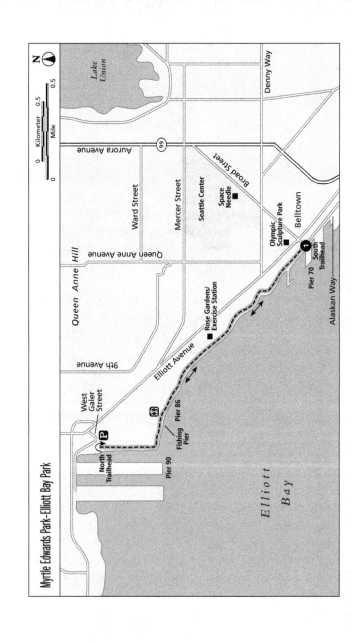

Myrtle Edwards Park–Elliott Bay Park

watch people pull in the catch of the day and where you'll
find restrooms, a water fountain, and vending machines.

The trail continues north along Pier 90's waterway to a
parking lot and the alternative (north) trailhead for this hike.
Turn around and retrace your steps to the starting point.

## Miles and Directions

**0.0** The south trailhead begins at Pier 70.

**1.7** Turn around at the parking lot and head in the opposite
direction.

**3.4** The trail ends back at Pier 70.

# 2 Alki Trail

Alki Beach is the birthplace of Seattle, where a schooner set the first settlers ashore in November 1851. Today, this long stretch of shoreline and beach in one of Seattle's liveliest and most scenic neighborhoods is where people come to play, dine, stroll, and scuba dive. If you've ever seen a postcard of Seattle's stunning skyline shot from across the harbor, the classic photo was likely taken from the starting point of this hike.

---

**Distance:** 4.6 miles out-and-back.
**Approximate hiking time:** 2–2.5 hours.
**Difficulty:** Moderate due to distance.
**Trail surface:** Paved.
**Best season:** Year-round.
**Other trail users:** Bicycles and skaters use a parallel trail.
**Canine compatibility:** Leashed dogs permitted.

**Fees and permits:** None required.
**Schedule:** Open daily, 24 hours a day.
**Maps:** Any Seattle street map, or USGS Seattle South W, WA and Seattle South E, WA.
**Trail contacts:** Seattle Parks and Recreation, (206) 684-4075, www.seattle.gov/parks

**Finding the trailhead:** From northbound or southbound Interstate 5, take exit 163 (West Seattle Bridge). Take the Harbor Ave. S.W. exit off the bridge and drive north on Harbor Ave. S.W. to Seacrest Park at 1660 Harbor Ave. S.W. Free parking is available in the lot or on the street. Summer season parking can be difficult. The trailhead GPS coordinates are: N47 35.35' / W122 22.89.'

# The Hike

The Alki Trail follows West Seattle's Harbor Ave. S.W. and Alki Ave. S.W. along Puget Sound in one of the city's most scenic areas. The trail passes through several parks, the largest of which is Alki Beach Park.

This hike takes in the most scenic segment of the trail, beginning at Seacrest Park, a spot popular with scuba divers, where you will find a pier, boathouse, restaurant, and restrooms. The focal point is the full frontal view of the Seattle skyline across Elliott Bay.

Walk north. You will soon pass Don Armeni Park and Boat Ramp and, beyond that, Duwamish Head where the trail veers to the left to round the head. The pier at Duwamish Head is a great place to pause and take in the view, which opens up at this point to include Puget Sound as it stretches north and Bainbridge Island and the Olympic Mountains (on a clear day) to the west.

After you've rounded Duwamish Head, the trail continues southwest along the seawall on Alki Ave. S.W., where, on the opposite side of the street, tiny beach cottages are nestled between modern luxury condos. At the beginning of the commercial district with its many restaurants, the seawall ends and the beach widens, allowing you a choice of hiking on pavement or sand. You will come to a community center building, a picnic shelter with several tables, and a miniature replica of the Statue of Liberty.

A short distance beyond, near the end of the public beach, a historical marker commemorates the spot where the Denny Party (Seattle's first European settlers) first came ashore on a stormy November day in 1851. This is the hike's turnaround point.

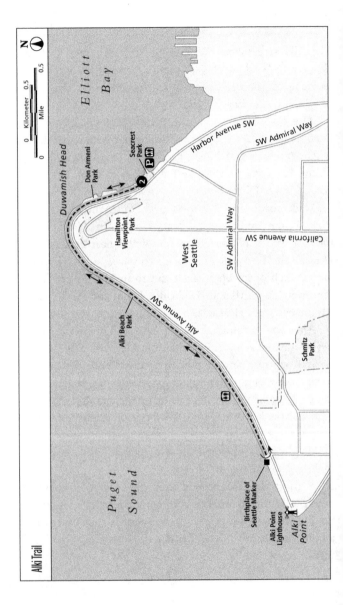

Alki Trail

Optionally, if you wish to add more miles of Puget Sound scenery to your hike, you can continue along Alki Ave. S.W. a few more blocks for views of the working lighthouse at Alki Point and even farther around the point for expansive views to the south across the Sound to Vashon Island. Or you can turn around at the Birthplace of Seattle marker and retrace your steps to your starting point at Seacrest Park.

## Miles and Directions

**0.0** The trail begins at Seacrest Park at 1660 Harbor Ave. S.W.; walk north toward Duwamish Head and Alki Beach.

**2.3** Turn around at the Birthplace of Seattle marker and return.

**4.6** The trail ends back at Seacrest Park.

# 3 Camp Long

Camp Long is a woodland retreat inside the Seattle city limits. This 68-acre park borders the West Seattle Golf Course and boasts miles of hiking trails, the first artificial climbing rock in North America, an environmental education center located in an old lodge, several rustic vacation rental cabins, and enough wildlife to attract hundreds of birders for an annual bird count.

**Distance:** 1.3-mile loop.
**Approximate hiking time:** 1 hour.
**Difficulty:** Moderate due to a 15% grade on sections of the trail and a 400-foot elevation gain.
**Trail surface:** Soil, gravel.
**Best season:** Year-round.
**Other trail users:** None.
**Canine compatibility:** Leashed dogs permitted.
**Fees and permits:** None required.

**Schedule:** Mar.-Oct.: open Tue.-Sun.; Nov.-Feb.: open Tue.-Sat. Hours: 10:00 a.m.-6:00 p.m.
**Maps:** Any Seattle street map; USGS Seattle South W, WA and Seattle South E, WA; or Camp Long trail map available at the park office.
**Trail contacts:** Seattle Parks and Recreation, (206) 684-4075, www.seattle.gov/parks

**Finding the trailhead:** From Interstate 5, take exit 163 (West Seattle Bridge). Stay on the bridge, which will become Fauntleroy Way S.W. Follow Fauntleroy as it curves to the left up the hill and turn left on 35th Ave S.W. (the first light). Take a left on Dawson Street to enter the park. The trailhead GPS coordinates are: N47 33.35' / W122 22.51'.

# The Hike

The creation of Camp Long began in 1937 and was a WPA project designed for public use as well as a Boy Scout retreat. Its mission was to bring people close to nature, one it has achieved many times over.

Before you begin your hike through Camp Long, stop at the information desk in the lodge and pick up a free park map. Although you'll find most of the trails well marked, a park map will help you navigate the few that aren't.

The trailhead begins at the right of the lodge. Head down the stairs to the Parade Ground and turn right. At the far end of the lawn you will pass a fire pit and beyond that you'll come to Schurman Rock, the first artificial climbing rock in North America, dedicated along with Camp Long in 1941. If you're a rock-climbing enthusiast, this is a rare opportunity to test your skill on a near antique.

Here you will turn right and follow the Longfellow Creek Trail into the forest and down the ravine. In just over 0.25 mile, you will come to a signed fork in the trail. Follow the Lower Loop Trail (straight ahead), which eventually begins to ascend. Several species are known to live in this forest, so be on the lookout for which ones you can spot.

At about 0.75 mile into the hike you will come to a wooden footbridge crossing Longfellow Creek on your right. Cross this bridge. In a short distance you will come to a convergence of trails with stairs straight ahead, another footbridge to the left, and an unmarked, well-maintained trail on your right (Animal Tracks Nature Trail) that continues up the hill. Take Animal Tracks Nature Trail. At the top of the hill, the trail will hairpin sharply to the left, and there you will find a bench. This is a peaceful place to catch your breath

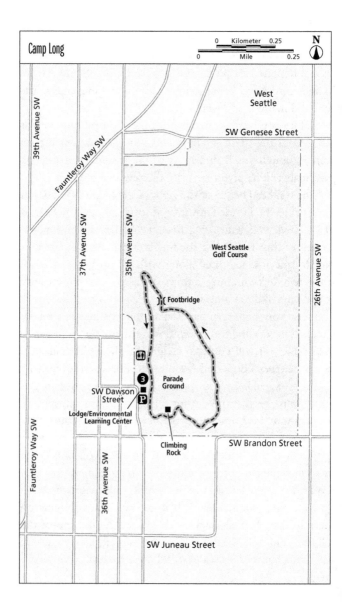

and enjoy the silence of the forest. You might even be lucky enough to spot one of the resident owls or an eagle.

Continuing on, you will come out of the forest and pass Polliwog Pond on the edge of the Parade Ground. At the center point of the Parade Ground, turn right and follow the stairs back up to the lodge and the trailhead.

## Miles and Directions

**0.0**  The trail begins immediately to the right of the lodge. Head down the stairs to the Parade Ground and turn right. Follow the trail around the lawn past the fire pit to Schurman Rock.

**0.2**  Turn right at Schurman Rock and follow the trail signs to Longfellow Creek Trail.

**0.5**  Follow the sign to Lower Loop Trail.

**0.7**  Turn right and cross the footbridge.

**0.8**  Turn right and follow Animal Tracks Nature Trail (unmarked).

**1.3**  The trail ends back at the lodge.

# $4$ Seward Park Loop

Seward Park juts into Lake Washington like a thumb. Seattle city officials had the foresight to acquire the wild, wooded property in 1892 and eventually turn it into the public space we enjoy today. The loop trail circles the park on a closed-off service road for most of its length, with the lake on one side and Seattle's largest remaining old-growth forest on the other.

---

**Distance:** 2.4-mile loop.
**Approximate hiking time:** 1 hour.
**Difficulty:** Easy, flat trail.
**Trail surface:** Paved.
**Best season:** Year-round.
**Other trail users:** Bicyclists, skaters.
**Canine compatibility:** Leashed dogs permitted.

**Fees and permits:** None required.
**Schedule:** Open daily, 6:00 a.m.–10:00 p.m.
**Maps:** Any Seattle street map, or USGS Seattle South E, WA and Bellevue South W, WA.
**Trail contacts:** Seattle Parks and Recreation, (206) 684-4075, www.seattle.gov/parks

---

**Finding the trailhead:** From Interstate 5, take exit 163 (S. Columbian Way). Follow S. Columbian Way to Beacon Ave. S., and turn right. Take the first left onto Orcas Ave. S. and follow it until it becomes Lake Washington Blvd. S. and, curving right, ends in Seward Park. The trailhead is beside the Art Studio building. The trailhead GPS coordinates are: N47 33.11' / W122 15.42'.

## The Hike

Lake Washington—a 20-mile-long lake lined with waterfront homes and parks—defines Seattle's eastern boundary. One of the city's most beautiful parks, Seward Park, occupies Bailey

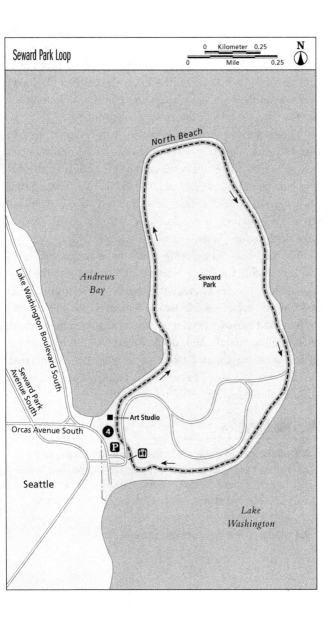

Seward Park Loop

Kilometer 0.25
Mile 0.25

N

North Beach

Andrews
Bay

Seward
Park

Lake Washington Boulevard South

Seward Park Avenue South

Orcas Avenue South

Art Studio

4

P

Seattle

Lake
Washington

Peninsula and is home to an environmental and Audubon center, a clay art studio, an amphitheater, picnic facilities, and miles of trails. The longest and most scenic of the park's trails is the Seward Park Loop (trail #10 on the park's official map, available on their website). This wide, paved trail doubles as a service road closed to motorized public traffic.

The trailhead for this hike begins at the edge of the lake near the art studio. As you skirt the edge of the peninsula, it's easy to forget you're still connected to the mainland; the setting has the distinctive feel of an island. In fact, Seward Park once was an island, and became attached to the mainland when the building of the locks on the ship canal lowered Lake Washington's water level.

The trail leads to a fishing pier, a wide swimming beach and lawn before rounding North Beach at the tip of the peninsula. Here, Mercer Island, with its luxury waterfront homes and forested hillside neighborhoods, comes into full view.

The trail narrows from a service road to a wide footpath in its ending stretch, and, if it's a clear day or at least one with a high enough cloud cover, you will be rewarded with an unobstructed view of massive Mt. Rainier dominating the horizon about seventy miles to the south.

## Miles and Directions

**0.0** There are two trailheads for the Seward Park Loop Trail, one at the parking lot at the end of Lake Washington Blvd. S. and the other at the Seward Park Art Studio. For the clockwise direction described in this chapter, the trail begins next to the Art Studio.

**2.4** The loop hike ends back at the trailhead.

# 5  Volunteer Park

Volunteer Park crowns Seattle's Capitol Hill, offering wind-
ing paths through lawns with formal gardens and a diverse
collection of mature trees—a prime example of elegant, early
landscape design—perfect for a slow stroll or a half-hour
hike. This popular city park is home to the Seattle Asian Art
Museum, the Volunteer Park Conservatory, and a brick water
tower that offers an unsurpassed 360° view of Seattle atop its
106 steps.

**Distance:** 1-mile loop.
**Approximate hiking time:**
.5 hour without visiting the
attractions.
**Difficulty:** Easy, flat and gently
sloped trail.
**Trail surface:** Paved, dirt.
**Best season:** Year-round.
**Other trail users:** Bicyclists,
skaters.

**Canine compatibility:** Leashed
dogs permitted.
**Fees and permits:** None
required.
**Schedule:** Open year-round, 6:00
a.m.–11:00 p.m.
**Maps:** Any Seattle street map, or
USGS Seattle North E, WA.
**Trail contacts:** Seattle Parks and
Recreation, (206) 684-4075,
www.seattle.gov/parks

**Finding the trailhead:** From downtown Seattle, drive east on Olive
Way over the Interstate 5 overpass. Follow E. Olive Way as it curves
to the right up the hill and becomes E. John St. Follow E. John St. to
Broadway E. and turn left. Turn right at E. Prospect, following the signs
to the Asian Art Museum. Take a left at 14th Ave. E. to enter Volunteer
Park. You can begin anywhere, but the suggested starting point is in
front of the Seattle Asian Art Museum. The trailhead GPS coordinates
are: N47 37.81' / W122 18.90'.

# The Hike

At the turn of the twentieth century, the City of Seattle hired the Olmsted Brothers, internationally renowned landscape architects, to design many of the city's parks. Volunteer Park was their crowning achievement in the city, integrating formal design elements with the natural environment.

Since this park is relatively small, you can easily explore it without a trail map or directions, but the prescribed route in this chapter circles the entire park in a short hike that allows you to take in the key attractions.

Begin your hike in front of the Asian Art Museum. Across the drive and parking lot, overlooking the city, you'll notice one of Seattle's classic postcard views: a black donut-shaped sculpture (Isamu Noguchi's "Black Sun") with the Space Needle, Puget Sound, and the Olympic Mountains in the distance.

Facing the museum, walk to the right, toward the water tower. Circle the tower and, before exiting the park, find the unpaved path on the left. Across the street sit some of Seattle's stateliest historic homes.

Turn left onto the path, which arcs down the hill and veers to the left (northward) through expansive sloping lawns and shade trees before heading back up the slope to the Conservatory. This structure, built in 1912, houses a vast collection of temperate, arid, and tropical plant specimens and is worth a visit (open 7 days a week, 10:00 a.m. until 4:00 p.m., and until 6:00 p.m. in the summer).

Facing the Conservatory, follow the unpaved path down the hill beside the drive, cross the drive, then descend the stairs to the left and follow the lawn below the drive. At the street, climb the stairs on the left, join the paved path beside

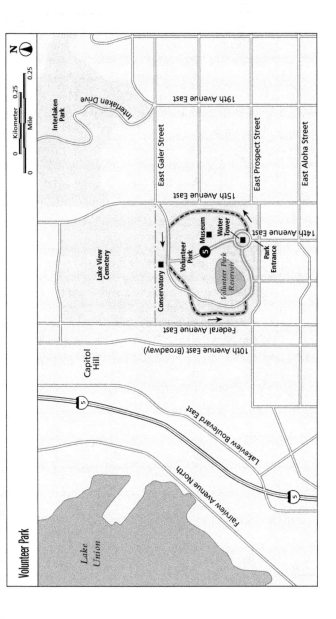

Volunteer Park

the drive, and follow the drive uphill toward the water tower. The reservoir, constructed in 1901, will be on your left.

The medieval-looking brick water tower rises above the highest point on one of Seattle's highest hills. For a free panorama that rivals a costly trip up the Space Needle, climb the water tower's 106 steps and savor the view of city, water, islands, and mountains.

Immediately to the north of the water tower, you will arrive back at the Seattle Asian Art Museum, a beautiful example of art deco architecture. Since this was a short hike, reward yourself with a tour of the museum (206-654-3100, www.seattleartmuseum.org/visit/visitSAAM.asp).

## Miles and Directions

**0.0** Begin in front of the Asian Art Museum; facing the museum, walk to the right (south) past the water tower and turn left onto the dirt path. The park is small enough to explore without a prescribed route, but if you circle the park close to the park boundaries, you will complete a 1-mile, half-hour hike.

**1.0** Arrive back at your starting point in front of the museum.

# 6 Green Lake

Green Lake Park is nestled in North Seattle's urban Green Lake neighborhood. The centerpiece of this 300-plus-acre park is the lake itself, which is surrounded by a 2.8-mile path. This popular park is one of the city's outdoor recreation hotspots and sits adjacent to Woodland Park, home of the Woodland Park Zoo.

**Distance:** 2.8-mile loop.
**Approximate hiking time:** 1.5 hours.
**Difficulty:** Easy, flat trail.
**Trail surface:** Paved and gravel.
**Best season:** Year-round.
**Other trail users:** Bicyclists, skaters, runners.
**Canine compatibility:** Leashed dogs permitted.

**Fees and permits:** None required.
**Schedule:** Open daily, 24 hours a day.
**Maps:** Any Seattle street map, or USGS Seattle North E, WA.
**Trail contacts:** Seattle Parks and Recreation, (206) 684-4075, www.seattle.gov/parks

**Finding the trailhead:** Because the Green Lake Trail is a loop, you can begin at any point. The following directions are for parking and beginning the hike at the south end of the lake. From Interstate 5, take exit 169 (N.E. 50th St. exit), turn left onto N.E. 50th St., turn right on Green Lake Way N., veer left onto W. Green Lake Way N., and park in the first lot on either side of the street just past the par 3 golf course. The trailhead GPS coordinates are: N47 40.32' / W122 20.62'

## The Hike

The same glacial ice sheet that scooped out Puget Sound also created Green Lake approximately 50,000 years ago.

Today, Green Lake occupies the bulk of a graceful city park containing an array of athletic and recreational facilities and a loop trail. You can begin the hike at any point on the trail, but for a frame of reference assume the trail begins at the Small Craft Center at the south end of the lake and that you will hike in a clockwise direction.

This easy 2.8-mile trail is one of the city's most popular spots for walking, jogging, and people-watching. It hugs the shore among rolling lawns, cattails, and a variety of mature shade trees, with pleasant views across the water to the park's greenery and the hillside neighborhoods beyond.

In just short of a mile, you will come to the Seattle Public Theater at the Bathhouse, an active stage theater housed in a converted 1928 bathhouse. A swimming beach is located behind the building.

At about the 1.8-mile mark, you will pass the Green Lake Park Community Center, complete with pool, indoor basketball court, athletic fields, tennis courts, boat rentals, concessions, swimming beach, rest rooms, and fishing dock.

Near the end of the loop, near the par 3 golf course, you will pass a piece of true Seattle kitsch: Green Lake Aqua Theater, the relic of a once 5,500-seat lakeside amphitheater circa 1950 that was home to an aquatic theater troop that performed lavishly staged "swimusicals"—musical theater complete with water ballet, high dives, and show tunes emanating from a floating orchestra pit (think Esther Williams films). Today, the portion of Aqua Theater that remains is part of the adjacent Small Craft Center. Round the bend a short distance and you are back at the starting point.

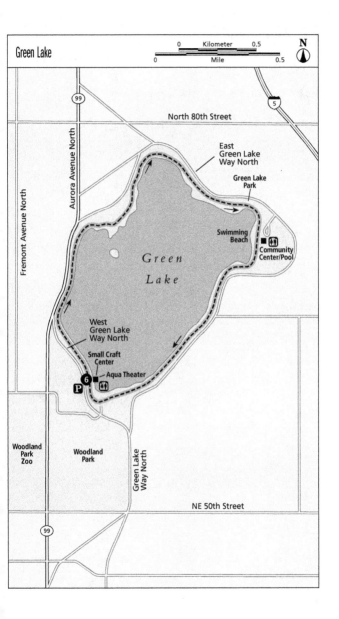

Green Lake

Kilometer  0
0.5

Mile  0
0.5

N

North 80th Street

99

Aurora Avenue North

Fremont Avenue North

East
Green Lake
Way North

Green Lake
Park

Green
Lake

Swimming
Beach

Community
Center/Pool

West
Green Lake
Way North

Small Craft
Center

Aqua Theater

6

P

Woodland
Park
Zoo

Woodland
Park

Green Lake
Way North

NE 50th Street

99

# Miles and Directions

**0.0**  Begin at the south end of the lake at the Small Craft Center; walk in either direction.

**2.8**  The loop trail ends back at starting point.

# 7  Discovery Park Loop Trail

Occupying 534 acres atop Seattle's Magnolia Bluff, Discovery Park is Seattle's largest. The first European ship to explore Puget Sound, Capt. George Vancouver's sloop *Discovery*, was the park's namesake. Hikers will discover nearly 12 miles of trails meandering through forests, open meadows, sand dunes, and sea cliffs, and to the West Point Lighthouse. The 2.8-mile Loop Trail offers sweeping views of Puget Sound, Alki Point, Vashon, Blakely, and Bainbridge Islands, and the Olympic Mountains. An optional spur trail follows Discovery Park Blvd. to the West Point Lighthouse and the beach, adding about 1 mile out and back for those who wish to extend the hike.

**Distance:** 2.8-mile loop.

**Approximate hiking time:** 1.5–2 hours.

**Difficulty:** Moderate due to a series of short hills.

**Trail surface:** Packed dirt, paved in a few short stretches.

**Best season:** Year-round.

**Other trail users:** Bicycles and skaters are permitted on paved sections only.

**Canine compatibility:** Leashed dogs permitted.

**Fees and permits:** None required.

**Schedule:** Open daily, 6:00 a.m.–11:00 p.m.

**Maps:** Any Seattle street map, or USGS Seattle North W, WA.

**Trail contacts:** Seattle Parks and Recreation, (206) 684-4075, www.seattle.gov/parks

**Finding the trailhead:** From downtown Seattle, drive west on Denny Way, which becomes Elliott Ave. and eventually 15th Ave. W.; take the Dravus St. exit and turn left at the light onto Dravus St.; turn right at 20th Ave. W., which becomes Gilman Ave. W. and eventually W. Government Way. The street ends at the entrance to the park. For easy access to the trail, park inside the park in the first lot on the left (east parking lot). The trail begins at the information kiosk. The trailhead GPS coordinates are: N47 39.50' / W122 24.35'

## The Hike

Discovery Park occupies the grounds of Fort Lawton, a former US military base, most of which has been acquired by the city of Seattle for public use. This large park encompasses a variety of terrain, and the well-maintained and heavily traveled Loop Trail passes through them all. This trail is clearly marked at intersections with minor trails and service roads, so if you follow the trail signs you can't go wrong.

Beginning your hike from the kiosk beside the east parking lot, in a counterclockwise direction, or north, you will immediately enter the forest and head up a gentle incline. For much of its length, the trail roller-coasters through a series of easy grades, but in a few short spots the trail is moderately steep (roughly a 10-15% grade), so trekking poles can be helpful.

Views throughout most of the hike are limited to the woods, hillsides, ravines, and the creatures that live there, so be on the lookout for bald eagles, great blue herons, woodpeckers, and many other species of birds.

About halfway through the hike, the trail approaches the edge of Magnolia Bluff, a 200-foot sea cliff. Here the expansive eagle's-nest view is breathtaking, and the open terrain of meadow and sand dunes ensures an unobstructed panorama. This is a great spot to linger and take in the ship and ferry traffic on the water below, or simply contemplate the natural beauty of the Puget Sound region. It's tempting to step up to the edge of the bluff, but be sure to observe the

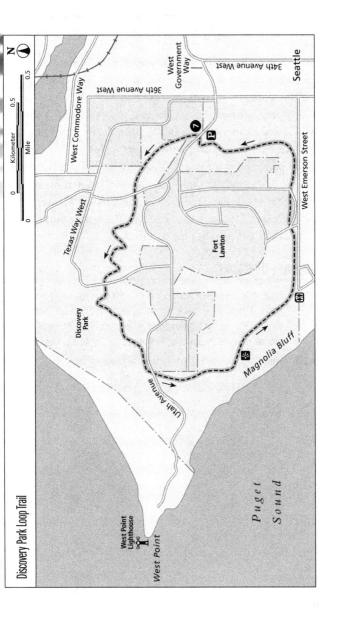

Discovery Park Loop Trail

warning signs and stay behind the designated area—the bluff is unstable and has been known to collapse.

When you're ready to tear yourself away from the view, the trail will lead you away from the bluff. The buildings on the hill ahead of you are remnants of the old military base, which was instrumental in housing troops in transit during WWII and also served as a POW camp during that same war.

The trail heads into the forest again along the south end of the park, and soon you will skirt the right edge of a parking lot (the south parking lot), so watch for trail markers indicating the Loop Trail and/or the Visitor's Center. They are the same trail and will lead you back to your starting point at the east parking lot trailhead.

## Miles and Directions

**0.0** Begin the hike at Discovery Park's east parking lot. The trailhead is located at the information kiosk near the entrance to the lot. Follow the sign indicating the Loop Trail. The trail is clearly marked throughout its length, so just follow the signs.

**2.8** The Loop Trail ends back at the east parking lot.

# 8  Cheshiahud Lake Union Loop

This 6-mile loop follows city streets around Lake Union, Seattle's central lake that borders downtown. The lake is a vibrant hub of activity, including boating, paddling, seaplanes, dining, and more. The hike passes through several neighborhoods, each offering the perfect excuse to rest or seek refreshments before continuing on to complete the loop.

**Distance:** 6.2-mile loop.
**Approximate hiking time:** 3 hours.
**Difficulty:** Moderate due to length.
**Trail surface:** Paved.
**Best season:** Year-round.
**Other trail users:** Bicycles.
**Canine compatibility:** Leashed dogs permitted.

**Fees and permits:** None required.
**Schedule:** Open daily, 4:00 a.m.–11:30 p.m.
**Maps:** Any Seattle street map, or USGS Seattle North.
**Trail contacts:** Seattle Parks and Recreation, (206) 684-4075, www.seattle.gov/parks

**Finding the trailhead:** The trail is accessible from many points around Lake Union. Suggested parking and trailhead are at Gasworks Park at the north end of the lake. To find Gasworks Park from Interstate 5, take the N.E. 45th St. exit, head west on N.E. 45th St., and turn left on Wallingford N.; it will end at Gasworks Park. The trailhead GPS coordinates are: N 47 38.79', W 122 20.10'.

## The Hike

Cheshiahud was Chief of the Duwamish Tribe village on Lake Union when settlers arrived and claimed the lake in 1853. The Duwamish village remained on Lake Union for another quarter of a century. This recently designated trail was named in the Chief's honor.

Gasworks Park on the north shore of Lake Union makes a perfect trailhead. From the park, follow the Burke-Gilman Trail to the west. The trail follows beside N. Northlake Way and passes under the Aurora Bridge before reaching the Fremont Bridge, the gateway to the quirky and eclectic Fremont neighborhood. (Those planning on doing some exploring along the route should detour in Fremont before returning to the trail.)

Cross the Fremont Bridge and follow Westlake Ave. N. along the western shore of Lake Union. The Westlake district is home to houseboats, marinas, a seaplane port, and several restaurants, making it a perfect spot to seek out a lakeside spot for refreshments.

At Lake Union Park, turn left through the park and pass the Museum of History and Industry. On the right is the South Lake Union district. The trail heads east through the park and along some piers with more eateries and viewpoints before joining the Fairview Walkway beside Fairview Ave. N. The Walkway will eventually turn into Fairview Ave. E. Follow Fairview Ave. E. past neighborhoods of houseboats in the Eastlake neighborhood.

At E. Roanoke St., Fairview Ave. E. ends temporarily. (You will rejoin it later.) Turn right onto E. Roanoke St., and in 1 block, turn left onto Yale Ave. E. Walk 1 block and turn right onto E. Edgar St. and then left on to Yale Terrace E. Turn left onto E. Hamlin St. and right onto the continuation of Fairview Ave E.

Follow Fairview Ave. E. past Fairview Park. The trail passes under the Ship Canal Bridge as it turns right onto

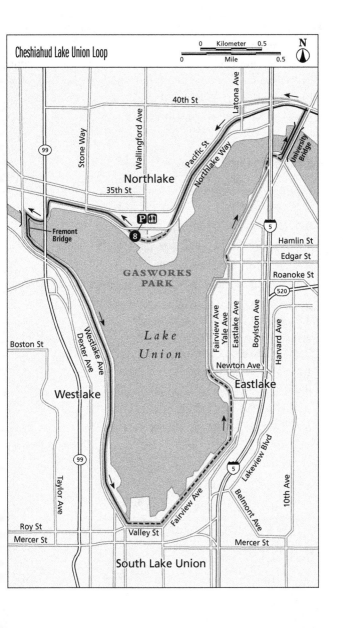

Cheshiahud Lake Union Loop

40th St

Latona Ave

Stone Way

Wallingford Ave

Pacific St

Northlake Way

Northlake

35th St

99

University Bridge

Fremont Bridge

P

8

5

Hamlin St

Edgar St

Roanoke St

GASWORKS PARK

520

Fairview Ave

Yale Ave

Eastlake Ave

Boylston Ave

Harvard Ave

Newton Ave

Lake Union

Eastlake

Westlake Ave

Dexter Ave

Boston St

Westlake

5

Lakeview Blvd

99

Taylor Ave

Fairview Ave

Belmont Ave

10th Ave

Roy St

Mercer St

Valley St

Mercer St

South Lake Union

N

Kilometer  0.5

Mile  0.5

Fuhrman Ave. E. Turn left onto Eastlake Ave. E. and cross the University Bridge.

At N.E. 40th St., exit Eastlake Ave. N.E. on the right, descend the stairs, cross beneath Eastlake Ave. N.E. and enter Peace Park. Follow the trail though the park until it once again joins the Burke-Gilman Trail. Follow the trail back to Gasworks Park.

## Miles and Directions

**0.0**  Begin the trail at Gasworks Park, which has parking, and head west.

**0.8**  Cross the Fremont Bridge.

**1.0**  Turn right onto Westlake Ave. E.

**2.4**  Enter Lake Union Park.

**2.6**  Turn left and follow the trail west along the south end of Lake Union.

**3.2**  Turn left to continue on Fairview Ave. E.

**4.1**  Turn right onto E Roanoke St. and follow the streets skirting the lake until you rejoin Fairview Ave. E.

**5.0**  Cross the University Bridge.

**5.2**  Exit Eastlake Ave NE, head west, follow the trail through Peace Park, and follow the Burke-Gilman Trail west.

**6.2**  The trail ends back at Gasworks Park.

# ⑨ Union Bay Natural Area

The University of Washington Botanical Gardens has set aside 74 acres as a wildlife refuge and a botanical field laboratory beside the Center for Urban Horticulture. Trails, wetlands, 4 miles of Lake Washington shoreline and habitat restoration projects make this a special spot for a short urban hike that is among the most interesting in Seattle.

**Distance:** 1-mile loop.
**Approximate hiking time:** 30 minutes.
**Difficulty:** Easy.
**Trail surface:** Gravel, dirt.
**Best season:** Year-round.
**Other trail users:** Foot traffic, bicycles.
**Canine compatibility:** Leashed dogs permitted.

**Fees and permits:** None required.
**Schedule:** Open daily, dawn to dusk.
**Maps:** Any Seattle street map, or USGS Seattle North.
**Trail contacts:** University of Washington, 206-543-8616, uwbg@uw.edu

**Finding the trailhead:** The trailhead is at the University of Washington Center for Urban Horticulture. To reach the trailhead from Interstate 5, take the N.E. 45th St. exit and drive east on N.E. 45th St. Turn right on Mary Gates Memorial Dr. N.E., which becomes N.E. 41st St. Turn right off N.E. 41st St. into the signed parking lot. The trailhead GPS coordinates are: N 4739.47', W 122 17.49'.

## The Hike

The loop trail through Union Bay Natural Area is a nature lover's hike. The Lake Washington shoreline plus wetlands teeming with waterfowl plus the restoration of native plants

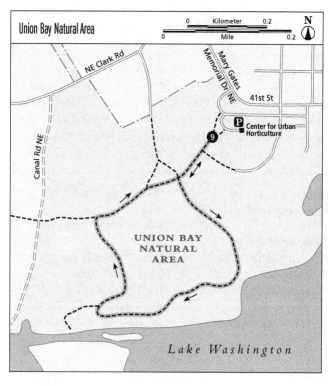

and wetlands in what was once a waste site and parking lot equal an environmental success story. It remains an important study site for the University of Washington College of the Environment.

The trailhead begins at the Center for Urban Horticulture parking lot. The trail is an easy loop. After entering the Natural Area on the trail, take the first left to begin the loop. The trail crosses open grasslands with views of the lake, Husky Stadium, and the university. Most of the trail remains in open areas and wetlands.

The trail traces the Lake Washington shoreline on your left and passes Central Pond on the right, a pond restoration project. It then veers to the right to skirt the UW wetlands before returning to the trailhead.

Birding in the Union Bay Natural Area is some of the best in the city with more than 200 species that either pass through or make the Natural Area their home. Birders should carry binoculars and pause to see what species they can spot.

Over time, the Union Bay Natural Area has been transformed from its original natural state to a waste repository and, finally, to the outdoor environmental laboratory it is today.

## Miles and Directions

**0.0** The trailhead begins at the parking lot.

**0.1** Turn left toward Lake Washington onto the loop trail.

**1.0** The trail ends back at the parking lot.

# 10 Washington Park Arboretum Loop Trail

Washington Park Arboretum is the crown jewel of Seattle parks, and it offers a recently completed loop trail to let urban hikers take it all in. The 230-acre park is home to more than 40,000 plant species in several groves and gardens. It is owned by the University of Washington and is co-managed by Seattle Parks and Recreation

**Distance:** 2-mile loop.
**Approximate hiking time:** 45 minutes.
**Difficulty:** Easy.
**Trail surface:** Paved.
**Best season:** Year-round.
**Other trail users:** Bicyclists.
**Canine compatibility:** Leashed dogs permitted.

**Fees and permits:** None required.
**Schedule:** Open daily, dawn to 8:00 p.m.
**Maps:** Any Seattle street map, or USGS Seattle North.
**Trail contacts:** Washington Park Arboretum, University of Washington, 206-543-8800, uwbg@uw.edu

**Finding the trailhead:** From Interstate 5, take the Madison St. exit; head east onto Madison St. and follow it just over 2 miles to Lake Washington Blvd. E. The trailhead is at the intersection of E. Madison St. and Lake Washington Blvd. E. Parking lots are available in the park but not at the trailhead. Street parking in the surrounding neighborhood is available. Metro Transit bus service is also available to the trailhead. The trailhead GPS coordinates are: N 47 37.59', W 122 17.55'.

# The Hike

For many Seattleites, the Washington Park Arboretum is a favorite. And its loop trail offers the perfect way to experience the best of the Arboretum. Its short length offers a quick, accessible break from city life. It's the perfect park for a rigorous walk or a slow stroll.

Begin the trail at the intersection of Madison St. and Lake Washington Blvd E. The trailhead is well marked, and the route is well signed along the way designating the Loop Trail from other intersecting pathways.

The first portion of the trail is built above and alongside Lake Washington Blvd E. and passes side trails to various gardens. The first, on the right, is the Pacific Connections Garden, featuring a collection of trees and plants from the more temperate regions of the Pacific Rim. Next, you'll pass Azalea Way, a springtime showpiece when the azaleas and rhododendrons, some the size of trees, are in bloom. Last, this stretch of the trail passes the Woodland Garden.

At about the halfway point the trail veers to the right. Turn right onto the road that leads to the Graham Visitor's Center, and veer right onto Arboretum Drive E., which returns to the trailhead. Along Arboretum Drive, side trails lead to the Witt Winter Garden, a must-see with blooming plants in the winter months. It also passes a meadow and Rhododendron Glen, a beautiful sunken garden with water features. Finally, just past the Pacific Connections Garden, the trail will rejoin the final stretch to the trailhead.

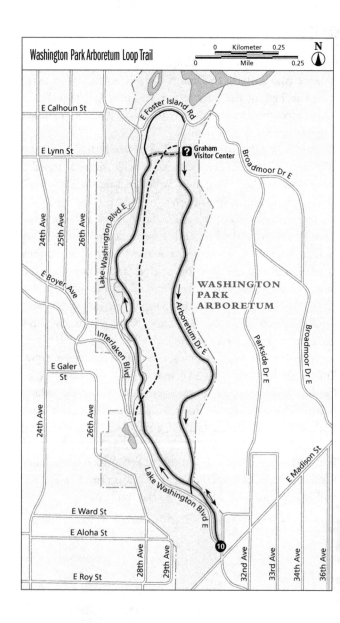

Washington Park Arboretum Loop Trail

E Calhoun St
E Foster Island Rd
E Lynn St

Graham
Visitor Center

Broadmoor Dr E

24th Ave
25th Ave
26th Ave

Lake Washington Blvd E

E Boyer Ave

WASHINGTON
PARK
ARBORETUM

Interlaken Blvd

Arboretum Dr E

E Galer
St

24th Ave

26th Ave

Parkside Dr E

Broadmoor Dr E

E Madison St

Lake Washington Blvd E

E Ward St

E Aloha St

28th Ave
29th Ave

E Roy St

32nd Ave
33rd Ave
34th Ave
36th Ave

10

N

0    Kilometer    0.25
0        Mile        0.25

## Miles and Directions

**0.0**  The trailhead begins at E. Madison St. and Lake Washington Blvd. E.

**1.0**  Turn right toward the Graham Visitor Center. At the Center, turn right onto Arboretum Dr. E.

**2.0**  The loop trail ends at the trailhead

# 11  Magnuson Park

Warren G. Magnuson Park occupies the site of the former Sand Point Naval Air Station on Lake Washington. When the base was closed, the city of Seattle acquired the land and buildings for public use and made good use of the waterfront and wide-open spaces for recreational and athletic facilities, including miles of trails. (As of the writing of this guidebook, large sections of the park were under renovation to restore wetlands and natural habitats as well as improve the athletic fields; when the project is completed, additional hiking trails will be available.)

**Distance:** 2.6 miles out-and-back with short loop.
**Approximate hiking time:** 1.5 hours.
**Difficulty:** Easy with one hill.
**Trail surface:** Paved, gravel.
**Best season:** Year-round.
**Other trail users:** Bicyclists, skaters.
**Canine compatibility:** Leashed dogs permitted; large off-leash area nearby.

**Fees and permits:** None required.
**Schedule:** Open year-round; May 1–Labor Day, 4:00 a.m.–11:30 p.m.; Labor Day–April 30, 4:00 a.m.–10:00 p.m.
**Maps:** Any Seattle street map, or USGS Seattle North E, WA and Bellevue North W, WA.
**Trail contacts:** Seattle Parks and Recreation, (206) 684-4075, www.seattle.gov/parks

**Finding the trailhead:** From downtown Seattle, drive north on Interstate 5 and take exit 169 (N.E. 45th St.). Turn right on N.E. 45th St. and follow it past the University of Washington and down the hill. The street will turn into Sandpoint Way N.E. and curve to the left. Turn right at N.E. 65th St., which ends at the Magnuson Park parking lot.

The trailhead is to the left of the boat ramp as you are facing the lake. The trailhead GPS coordinates are: N47 40.55' / W122 15.04'.

## The Hike

Lake Washington stretches 20 miles along Seattle's entire eastern border and beyond, its shoreline home to miles of promenades, parks, bicycle trails, waterfront homes, neighborhood commercial districts, a hydroplane racing pit, the on-ramps of two floating bridges and even the site of a former naval air station. When the Sand Point Naval Air Station closed, the city of Seattle seized the opportunity to acquire the lakefront property to create Magnuson Park, which now shares Sand Point with the National Oceanographic and Atmospheric Administration (NOAA).

Magnuson Park contains miles of trails. This hike follows the lakefront promenade, ascends Sand Point Head (a.k.a. Kite Hill), and circles a hilltop field with excellent views up and down the lake, east to the city of Kirkland and beyond to the Cascade Mountains.

About midway along the promenade, you will notice something resembling killer whale dorsal fins—twenty-two of them in all—breaching the lawn as it gently rolls like waves. These are actually black diving fins from decommissioned Navy attack submarines buried in the hillside, making up a provocative art installation titled "The Fin Project."

The promenade ends at a gate leading to a high point of the hike for your canine companion, if you brought one: an enormous, fenced, off-leash area that meanders through the park. This optional delight for your dog will temporarily take you off the trail, but you can backtrack and easily find the gate again and continue up Kite Hill to resume the hike.

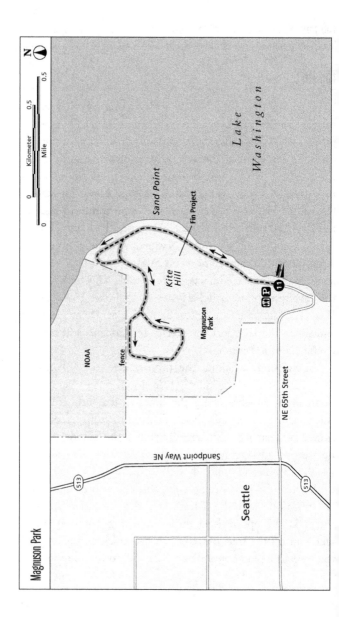

## Magnuson Park

N

Kilometer
0        0.5

Mile
0        0.5

Lake Washington

Sand Point

Fin Project

Kite Hill

Magnuson Park

NOAA

fence

11

Sandpoint Way NE

NE 65th Street

Seattle

513

An optional nearby attraction resides on the secured grounds of NOAA: a lakefront Art Walk. One of the highlights of the collection is a sculptural installation titled "Sound Garden," a collection of pipes that play eerie sounds in the wind, the tone and pitch determined by the wind's direction and velocity. To access Art Walk, go to the NOAA security gate on 63rd Ave. N.E., immediately to the north of the park, and request access to the Art Walk. If the current security level permits, you will go through a routine security screening, then be issued a visitor's pass and permitted to enter.

## Miles and Directions

**0.0** Begin hike at the lakeside promenade next to the boat launch at the park's south parking lot; cross the footbridge and follow the promenade north.

**0.4** The trail passes "The Fin Project," an art installation.

**0.7** The trail reaches the off-leash area for dogs and turns to the left along the fence.

**0.8** At the trail intersection, turn right and follow the trail up Kite Hill and beyond to the athletic fields. Circle the field for great views of the park, and take the same trail back down the hill.

**1.9** Walk straight through the trail intersection toward the lake.

**2.0** Turn right at the lakeside promenade and walk south toward the trailhead.

**2.6** Arrive back at the trailhead.

# 12 Lakeridge Park (Deadhorse Canyon)

Hiking the trail up the ravine and back down, it's easy to lose sight of the fact that you are in the middle of a city. The trail is popular with native plant enthusiasts, birders, and neighborhood residents walking their dogs or just out for some exercise. Why was its original name "Deadhorse Canyon?" The area was logged for timber around the turn of the 20th century; some say it was named after a logging term for fallen trees that were not removed. Others claim it was named after a beloved horse that would roam the canyon and, yes, died.

**Distance:** 0.8 mile out-and-back.

**Approximate hiking time:** 45 minutes.

**Difficulty:** Moderate, with a 144-foot elevation gain.

**Trail surface:** Dirt and wooden bridges.

**Best season:** Year-round.

**Other trail users:** Foot traffic only.

**Canine compatibility:** Leashed dogs permitted.

**Fees and permits:** None required.

**Schedule:** Open daily, 4:00 a.m.–11:30 a.m.

**Maps:** Any Seattle street map, or USGS Mercer Island.

**Trail contacts:** Seattle Parks and Recreation, (206) 684-4075, https://www.seattle.gov/parks

**Finding the trailhead:** From Rainier Avenue South in South Seattle, turn onto 68th Avenue S. In less than .25 mile, trailhead parking will be on 68th Avenue S. as it becomes Holyoke Way S. Parking spaces are limited. *Note:* Do not park at Lakeridge Playfield; there is no access to the trail from there. Trailhead GPS coordinates are: N47 30.52', W122 14.89'.

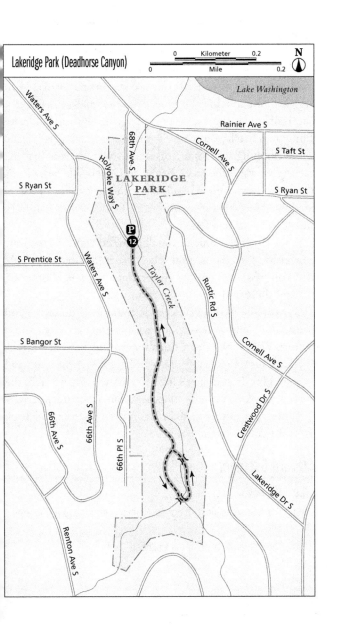

Lakeridge Park (Deadhorse Canyon)

Kilometer 0.2
Mile 0.2

N

Lake Washington
Rainier Ave S
Cornell Ave S
S Taft St
Waters Ave S
68th Ave S
Holyoke Way S
LAKERIDGE PARK
S Ryan St
S Ryan St
Waters Ave S
S Prentice St
Taylor Creek
Rustic Rd S
S Bangor St
Cornell Ave S
66th Ave S
66th Ave S
66th Pl S
Crestwood Dr S
Lakeridge Dr S
Renton Ave S

# The Hike

Taylor Creek tumbles down Deadhorse Canyon (aka Lakeridge Park) with both sides of the ravine blanketed in a thick forest of native vegetation and second-growth trees. The trail traces the creek up the ravine with a moderate climb on a well-maintained path. It levels off periodically before climbing again and crosses a few wooden foot bridges, offering views of the creek below and creek-side vegetation. Along the way, pause to look up at the specimens of native trees, including bigleaf maple, cedar, Douglas and grand firs, and alder, to name a few.

After about 0.3 mile, you will come to a fork in the trail. Take either path, as the trail splits here into a loop. Any side trails you pass leads up into the surrounding neighborhoods, so avoid those and stay on the main trail.

As you follow the trail, keep in mind that the ravine and surrounding land were teeming with logging activity around the turn of the 20th century, and a sawmill was once onsite. With the lush vegetation, the stands of towering trees, and no sound but birdsong, it's hard to envision. Fortunately, the ravine was spared from development due to the steep terrain.

When you return to the fork in the trail, follow it back down the ravine to the trailhead.

## Miles and Directions

**0.0** The trail begins.

**0.3** The trail splits into a loop; take either path to loop at the top of the trail.

**0.8** The trail ends back at the trailhead.

# 13 Sammamish River–Burke–Gilman Trails: Bothell Landing

Bothell Landing on the north bank of the Sammamish River is a quaint step back in time. This park contains one of the first pioneer cabins in the area and a collection of later Victorian homes that now house a historical museum and an event space. A footbridge crosses the river to the 11-mile Sammamish River Trail, which hikers can follow in either direction. This hike follows a short segment of the trail along the river to the right.

**Distance:** 3.4 miles out-and-back.

**Approximate hiking time:** 1.5 hours.

**Difficulty:** Easy, flat trail with a few gentle inclines.

**Trail surface:** Paved.

**Best season:** Year-round.

**Other trail users:** Bicyclists, skaters.

**Canine compatibility:** Leashed dogs permitted.

**Fees and permits:** None required.

**Schedule:** Open year-round; Bothell Landing hours: 8:00 a.m. to dusk.

**Maps:** Any King Co. street map, or USGS Bothell, WA.

**Trail contacts:** City of Bothell Parks and Recreation, (425) 486-7430, www.ci.bothell.wa.us/dept/parks/parksindex.html; King County Parks and Recreation, (206) 296-8687, www.kingcounty.gov/recreation/parks.aspx

**Finding the trailhead:** From downtown Seattle, drive north on Interstate 5 and take exit 177 (Lake Forest Park). Turn right after the exit and follow Highway 104 to Lake Forest Park. At Lake Forest Park Center, turn left onto Bothell Way. N.E. (S.R. 522), follow it through Kenmore, and turn right at 180th St. N.E. Drive one block and turn right into the Park at Bothell Landing; the trail begins at the footbridge. The trailhead GPS coordinates are: N47 45.49' / W122 12.46'.

## The Hike

The Sammamish River meanders through north King County, flowing from Lake Sammamish to Lake Washington, the two large lakes to the east of Seattle. The trail's 11 miles make up a small fraction of the extensive Regional Trail System in King County and can be accessed from many points.

For a perfect short hike, begin at the Park at Bothell Landing, with its collection of historic buildings and its nineteenth century village feel. Take the footbridge across the river and begin your hike to the right. As you enjoy this riverbank trail, keep an eye out for the variety of waterfowl that frequent the river.

The trail follows the south riverbank through woods and grassy slopes, crosses the river again on another footbridge, follows the north bank for a distance, and then divides. This fork marks the end of the Sammamish River Trail and the beginning of the roughly 18-mile Burke-Gilman Trail that heads into Seattle.

The left fork crosses a footbridge to Blyth Park and Norway Hill where it joins the western trailhead of the 14-mile Tolt Pipeline Trail to the east toward the Cascade foothills. Take the right fork (the Burke-Gilman Trail) and follow it through the underpass and along the easement beside the Wayne Golf Course. This stretch of the trail overlooks the greens, the park-like grounds of the course, and the river meandering below.

After the golf course, the trail passes by a riverside residential area on the left and Highway 522 above the retaining wall on the right. As the trail gets closer to the highway, traffic noise and roadside businesses interfere with the countryside ambience of the hike, so this is a good place to turn around and retrace your steps to Bothell Landing. Or you may choose to turn this into a longer hike and continue onward a few more miles through the city of Kenmore to where the trail meets Lake Washington.

On the hike back to Bothell Landing, you may take an alternate route where the Burke-Gilman Trail becomes the Sammamish River Trail (after the underpass), and, instead of taking the Sammamish River Trail to the left, take the right fork across the old trestle. As you approach Blyth Park, take the first path on the left (across the trail from the park) paralleling the Sammamish River Trail on the hillside. Turn left at the first junction, a paved trail that rejoins the Sammamish River Trail. Turn right onto the Sammamish River Trail and follow it back to the Park at Bothell Landing.

## Miles and Directions

**0.0**  At Bothell Landing, take the footbridge over the river and follow the trail to the right along the river.

**0.5**  The Sammamish River Trail ends and the Burke-Gilman Trail begins at a fork in the trail; take the right fork through the underpass (Burke-Gilman Trail).

**1.7**  Turn around before you reach Highway 522 and retrace your steps.

**2.7**  For a short alternate route back, take the right fork at the end of the Burke-Gilman Trail, cross the footbridge across the river, take the first path to the left (across the trail from Blyth Park).

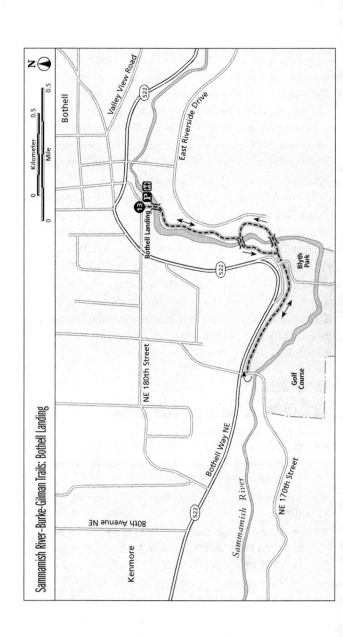

Sammamish River–Burke-Gilman Trails: Bothell Landing

**2.9** Turn left at the first trail junction. This paved trail descends the hill and joins the Sammamish River Trail.

**3.0** Turn right onto the Sammamish River Trail.

**3.4** Arrive back at the trailhead at the Park at Bothell Landing.

# 14 Soos Creek Trail

The Puget Sound Basin is laced with wetlands, many accessible by some excellent, well-maintained trails. Soos Creek is a prime example of a wetland ecosystem in which the creek feeds ponds and swamps and supports a rich diversity of plant and animal life. A multi-use trail extends more than 7 miles one-way beside the creek; this hike explores the northern segment of that trail.

**Distance:** 5.0 miles out-and-back.

**Approximate hiking time:** 2–2.5 hours.

**Difficulty:** Moderate due to distance and a few gradual inclines.

**Trail surface:** Paved.

**Best season:** Year-round.

**Other trail users:** Bicyclists, skaters, equestrians (on the soft surface shoulder and parallel horse trail).

**Canine compatibility:** Leashed dogs permitted.

**Fees and permits:** None required.

**Schedule:** Open year-round, dawn to dusk.

**Maps:** Any South King County. street map, or USGS Renton, WA.

**Trail contacts:** King County Parks and Recreation, (206) 296-8687, www.kingcounty.gov/recreation/parks.aspx

**Finding the trailhead:** From Seattle, drive south on Interstate 5. Take exit 152 (S. 188th St./Orillia Rd. S.) and turn left on S. 188th St., which immediately curves right onto Orillia Rd. S. Follow Orillia Rd. S. down the hill; it will curve left and become S. 212th St. Follow this street through the valley, under the Highway 167 overpass, and up the hill where it becomes S. 208th St. Turn left into the signed parking lot at Soos Creek Park. The north trailhead GPS coordinates are: N47 24.97' / W122 9.56'.

# The Hike

A long stretch of Soos Creek—an important tributary of the Duwamish and Green River Watershed—is bordered by a wide greenbelt of wetlands that has been set aside as a county park with a paved multi-use trail. This trail offers an excellent opportunity to explore a natural wetland environment without traveling far from the city.

The trail begins at Soos Creek Park, which has parking, restrooms, a picnic shelter, and children's play area. A short spur of the Soos Creek Trail heads north through the park and dead-ends in 0.5 mile. Instead, for a longer hike through the wetlands, cross the street and the footbridge and head south on the paved trail.

At first the trail cuts a path close to pastures and stables, but soon the wetlands expand and the landscape is rich with cattails, alders, and other wetland vegetation above the surface of the water and plants such as water parsley below. The branches here are heavy with moss, and opportunistic ferns set down roots wherever they can. This trail is popular with birders for a reason; watch for waterfowl, hawks, and other birds that make the wetlands their home.

At the half-mile point, the trail crosses a street; at the 1-mile point, a country road interrupts the trail, but the trail resumes across the road about 450 feet to the right. Here the trail follows some power lines for about .25 of a mile, but never leaves the wetlands. The trail then heads up and down a few gentle slopes as it enters a riparian forest that overlooks the creek below.

You will eventually hear but not see evidence of civilization again with the roar of a highway just up the ridge. When you come to the next road, you can turn around and retrace

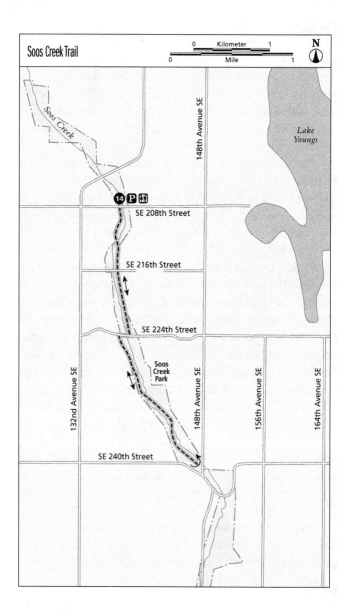

your steps back to the trailhead to complete the 5-mile round-trip hike, or you can cross the road and continue on to add more mileage.

## Miles and Directions

**0.0** The north trailhead begins across the street from the park. Cross the street and continue south across the footbridge.

**0.5** The trail crosses another street.

**1.0** You will come to a rural road. Turn right onto the road, walk 450 feet, and turn left onto the trail, which is well marked.

**2.5** Turn around and retrace your steps to the trailhead. For a longer hike (more than twice the length, round-trip), continue to the south end of the trail, where you will turn around and return to the north trailhead.

**5.0** Arrive back at the north trailhead.

# 15 Pioneer Park

This oasis on Mercer Island in Lake Washington provides a vast greenspace that belies its urban setting. The park is criss-crossed with 6.6 miles of trails through a variety of terrains, so hikers can easily customize their outing. Popular with walkers, joggers, birders, and even equestrians (on designated routes), trails traverse fern- and moss-laden forests, ravines, and flatlands.

**Distance:** 1.8-mile loop.
**Approximate hiking time:** 1 hour.
**Difficulty:** Easy to moderate; trail descends and ascends a ravine with an elevation gain of approx. 80 feet.
**Trail surface:** Dirt, gravel.
**Best season:** Year-round.
**Other trail users:** Foot traffic; bicycles and equestrians are allowed on designated trails.

**Canine compatibility:** Leashed dogs permitted.
**Fees and permits:** None required.
**Schedule:** Open daily, 24 hours a day.
**Maps:** Any Seattle street map, or USGS Mercer Island, WA.
**Trail contacts:** City of Mercer Island Parks and Recreation, (206) 275-7600, https://www .mercerisland.gov/parksrec

**Finding the trailhead:** Pioneer Park has several trailheads with on-street parking and near bus stops. The trailhead for the trail route described in this chapter is located at the northwest corner of the northwest quadrant of the park at the intersection of 84th Ave. S.E. and S.E. 64th St. Mercer Island. You will drive onto Mercer Island from Interstate 90; take the Island Crest Way exit, and drive south on Island Crest Way approximately 4 miles. The trailhead GPS coordinates are: N47 32.74', W122 13.62'.

# The Hike

Pioneer Park on Mercer Island is divided into three quadrants, each separated by city streets. The City of Mercer Island purchased this 113-acre tract of forested land to protect it from development and set it aside as a green oasis for wildlife and people. Later, the Mercer Island Open Space Conservancy Trust acquired the park. The trail route selected for this hike explores the northwest and northeast quadrants of the park. The southeast quadrant is designated for equestrian use but is open to foot traffic as well.

The trails in Pioneer Park are named and signed, so it's easy to follow any planned route. The route recommended here begins on the Northwest Perimeter Trail and follows the Overlook Trail, Ravine Trail, Chickadee Trail, Alder Trail, and Dogwood Trail—offering varied aspects of the park's terrain and vegetation.

The Northwest Perimeter Trail begins in a forest dominated by deciduous trees with some evergreens mixed in. If you're hiking with your canine best friend, the northwest quadrant is an off-leash area. Cross this quadrant on the Northwest Perimeter Trail and cross the street to the northeast quadrant. Here the terrain becomes more varied with ridges, steep ravines, running streams, and generally more ecological variety. Upon entering the northeast quadrant, follow the Overlook Trail and then the Ravine Trail, both aptly named. The Ravine Trail will descend into a ravine and ascend with approximately 80 feet of elevation gain. Take the Chickadee Trail and cross the street again back to the northwest quadrant and follow the Northwest Perimeter, Alder, and Dogwood trails back to your starting point.

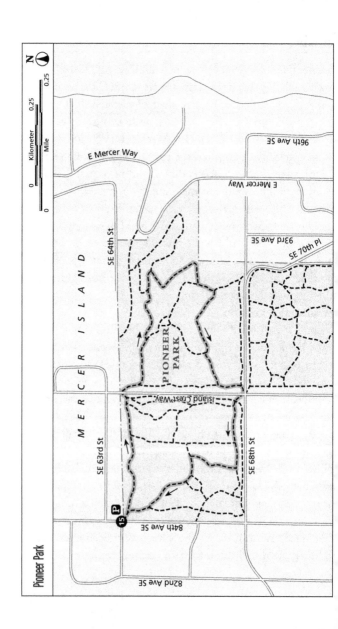

Pioneer Park

# Miles and Directions

**0.0** The trail begins at the northwest corner of the northwest quadrant; follow Northwest Perimeter Trail to the left.

**0.6** Cross Island Crest Way turn right on the Bike Trail.

**0.7** Turn left onto Overlook Trail, and in a short distance, veer left onto Ravine Trail.

**1.2** Turn left onto Overlook Trail.

**1.3** Turn left onto Chickadee Trail and soon turn left onto Bike Trail; cross Island Crest Way and follow the Northwest Perimeter Trail to the left.

**1.4** Turn right on Alder Trail.

**1.6** Turn left onto Woodpecker Trail.

**1.7** Turn right onto Dogwood Trail and in a short distance turn right onto Northwest Perimeter Trail.

**1.8** Return to the trailhead.

# 16  Mercer Slough Nature Park

The largest wetlands on the shores of Lake Washington have been preserved as Mercer Slough Nature Park. The park's well-maintained interpretive trails provide easy access to this important wildlife habitat. Day hikers not only enjoy the outdoors but also learn about wetland wildlife, the fascinating history of the area's early settlers, and the only operating blueberry farm in the vicinity.

**Distance:** 2.1-mile double loop.
**Approximate hiking time:** 1 hour.
**Difficulty:** Easy, flat trail.
**Trail surface:** Raised boardwalk, bark chips, dirt.
**Best season:** Year-round.
**Other trail users:** None.
**Canine compatibility:** Leashed dogs permitted.

**Fees and permits:** None required.
**Schedule:** Open year-round; dawn to dusk.
**Maps:** Any Bellevue street map, or USGS Bellevue South W, WA.
**Trail contacts:** Bellevue Parks, (425) 452-6885, www.ci.bellevue.wa.us/parks_homepage.htm

**Finding the trailhead:** From Seattle, drive east on Interstate 90, and take exit 9 (Bellevue Way S.E.). Drive north on Bellevue Way S.E. and watch for the Winters House sign on the right. Turn right into the parking lot. The trailhead begins behind the Winters House. The trailhead GPS coordinates are: N47 35.49' / W122 11.58'.

## The Hike

In 1856, Native American tribes assembled at a place called sa'tsakal to organize an assault on the pioneer settlement of Seattle. That staging ground was located at present-day Mercer Slough, and the skirmish, a failed protest over treaty terms, would later become known as the Battle of Seattle. Today, the city of Bellevue surrounds Mercer Slough and the vast natural wetlands that border it, a habitat for more than 170 species of wildlife.

Start your hike on the Heritage Trail behind Winters House. This trail begins on a long raised boardwalk over the bogs and wetlands and eventually becomes a bark-chip trail following the edge of a working blueberry farm. The trail soon reaches the slough and crosses the Slough Channel Bridge—a footbridge that's a great place to pause and see how many species of waterfowl you can spot.

On the other side of the slough, the Bellefields Loop Trail begins on the left and switches between a boardwalk and soft-surface trail with wetland interpretive displays along the route. Follow this trail to the left for a clockwise hike through wetlands, into an upland forest, down through wetlands again and back to the Slough Channel Bridge. A few unmarked trail junctions can make the Bellefields Loop Trail confusing, but if you remember that when in doubt you should follow the right-hand fork for a clockwise loop, you won't go wrong. The only exception is at the end of the loop, where a left turn onto the raised boardwalk leads you back to the Slough Channel Bridge.

Across the bridge, rejoin the Heritage Trail. Immediately on the left, a short spur to a viewing deck provides a quiet spot to rest and observe wetland life. As you continue on the Heritage Trail, the modern high-rises of downtown Bellevue come into view on one side and the summit of Mt. Rainier on the other. Follow the trail signs back to the Winters House.

The Mercer Slough Environmental Education Center, not on this hike's route, is located across the park at the 118th

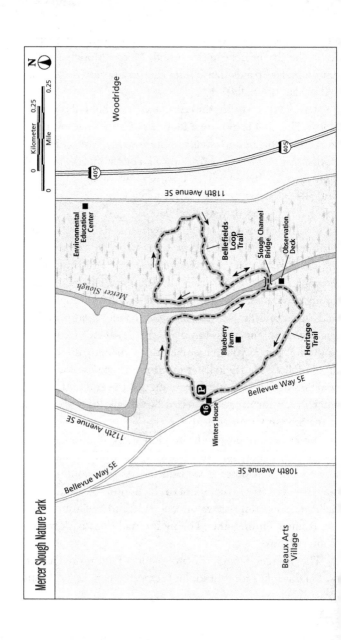

Mercer Slough Nature Park

Ave S.E. entrance. Great for kids and adults, it's worth a visit for the interpretive displays about the wetlands and local history, nature art exhibits, and educational programs. A quick visit prior to hitting the trail can make your hike through Mercer Slough Nature Park a more informed experience.

## Miles and Directions

**0.0**   The trail begins behind the Winters House.

**0.5**   Turn left at the trail intersection, cross the Slough Channel Bridge (footbridge), and follow the raised boardwalk to the left (Bellefields Trail).

**0.7**   The trail will fork; follow the left fork for a clockwise loop on the Bellefields Trail.

**1.0**   You will come to an unsigned junction. Follow the trail on the right.

**1.1**   You will come to another unsigned junction. Follow the trail on the right.

**1.3**   At the trail junction, follow the trail on the right directing you to Slough Channel Bridge.

**1.4**   At the trail junction, turn left and follow the trail on the raised boardwalk.

**1.5**   Cross the Slough Channel Bridge and turn left for a short spur trail to an observation platform. Back at the main trail, turn left.

**1.6**   At the trail junction, turn right and follow the trail back to Winters House and the trailhead.

**2.1**   Arrive back at the trailhead.

# 17 Cougar Mountain Regional Wildland Park: Red Town–Wildside Trails

Cougar Mountain stands as the westernmost of the Issaquah Alps, what remains of a mountain range that geologically predates the nearby Cascades. With more than 3,000 acres and 36 miles of hiking trails at all levels of difficulty, Cougar Mountain Regional Wildland Park reigns as the king of King County Parks.

**Distance:** 1.7-mile loop.
**Approximate hiking time:** 1–1.5 hours.
**Difficulty:** Moderate due to several short hills with more than a 100-foot elevation gain.
**Trail surface:** Dirt and gravel.
**Best season:** Year-round, but trails are muddy after a rain.
**Other trail users:** Equestrians on portions of the trail.

**Canine compatibility:** Leashed dogs permitted.
**Fees and permits:** None required.
**Schedule:** Open year-round; hours: 8:00 a.m. to dusk.
**Maps:** Any King Co. street map, or USGS Issaquah, WA.
**Trail contacts:** King County Parks and Recreation, (206) 296-8687, www.kingcounty.gov/recreation/parks.aspx

**Finding the trailhead:** From Seattle, drive east on Interstate 90 and take exit 13 (Lakemont Blvd. S.E.). Follow Lakemont Blvd. S.E. until you come to a sign on the left for the Red Town Trail. Turn into the parking lot. All the trails in the park are well signed. The trailhead GPS coordinates are: N47 32.09' / W122 7.74'.

# The Hike

The Seattle region's coal mining past largely lies hidden beneath the forest floor on the western slopes of Cougar Mountain. If it weren't for a few preserved artifacts and interpretive kiosks, hikers on the mountain's trails would remain clueless that less than a hundred years ago, a vast coal mining operation and a community of miners and their families— Red Town, a neighborhood of nearby Newcastle—occupied the mountainside where lush forest now stands. In less than a century, nature has completely reclaimed the mountain.

Red Town Trail, basically a gravel and dirt service road, leaves the parking lot on a gradual ascent. Hikers pass the junction to the more difficult Cave Hole Trail and several smaller spur trails, perhaps considerations for future hiking trips to this large, close-to-civilization park. Red Town Trail eventually narrows and becomes Indian Trail at a junction with an optional side path, which passes a meadow restoration project with information posted about the project and the history of Red Town.

To complete the loop, transfer to Marshall's Hill Trail and then, after a short distance, to Wildside Trail, which winds and rolls gently through the thick forest.

Near the end of the loop, a short spur leads to Ford Slope Mine where you will see the sealed entrance to the coal mine with a rusty air vent still protruding from the ground. A nearby steam hoist—its foundation still in the forest—lowered the miners more than 1,700 feet into the mine shaft, which bottoms out 200 feet below sea level, and hauled the coal out. An excellent kiosk display of historic photos of miners waiting to be lowered into the mine at the very spot where you are standing breathes life into the site. Other

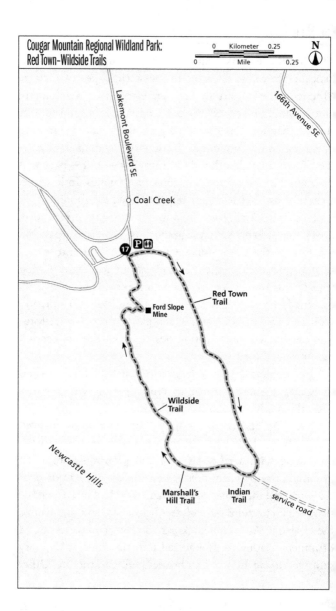

Cougar Mountain Regional Wildland Park:
Red Town–Wildside Trails

0    Kilometer    0.25
0    Mile    0.25

N

Lakemont Boulevard SE

166th Avenue SE

Coal Creek

17  P

Red Town
Trail

Ford Slope
Mine

Wildside
Trail

Newcastle Hills

Marshall's
Hill Trail

Indian
Trail

service road

captioned photos of the mining operation, the town, and the miners and their families round out the experience.

When you hike Cougar Mountain, trekking poles are useful to help negotiate the few slopes and the slippery trail surfaces after a rain. Although the park's trails are well signed, due to the number of trails and trail junctions, a park map can come in handy. Also, it is crucial to stay on the trails. The former mining operation scarred Cougar Mountain with possible hazards, such as unstable ground, the potential of collapsing mine shafts, and hidden mining hardware.

## Miles and Directions

**0.0** From the parking lot, begin on the Red Town Trail, which is a wide gravel and dirt service road to the left of the kiosk, and follow it up the hill.

**0.8** Red Town Trail ends and becomes Indian Trail. At this signed junction an alternate trail goes past the Meadow Restoration Project and joins the main trail again in a short distance. Just past the Indian Trail trailhead, you will come to another signed junction; leave Indian Trail and follow Marshall's Hill Trail straight ahead.

**1.0** Walk through the wooden equestrian barrier and onto Wildside Trail (straight ahead).

**1.5** Follow the short spur to Ford Slope Mine where you will find historic information and mining relics.

**1.7** Arrive back at the trailhead.

# 18 Squak Mountain

Squak Mountain has been preserved as a vast, wooded state park that's just minutes from Seattle. Its trails range from easy to difficult, but all have one thing in common: They share a quintessential Pacific Northwest forest that's closed to all activity except hiking, running, and, on designated trails, horseback riding (so watch your step).

**Distance:** 3.4-mile loop.
**Approximate hiking time:** 2.5 hours.
**Difficulty:** More challenging due to a 700-foot elevation gain and loss.
**Trail surface:** Dirt and gravel.
**Best season:** Year-round.
**Other trail users:** Equestrians on segments of the trail.
**Canine compatibility:** Leashed dogs permitted.

**Fees and permits:** None required.
**Schedule:** Open all year; summer hours: 6:30 a.m.–dusk; winter hours: 8:00 a.m.–dusk.
**Maps:** Any King Co. street map, or USGS Maple Valley, WA.
**Trail contacts:** Washington State Parks, (360) 902-8844, www .parks.wa.gov

**Finding the trailhead:** From Interstate 90, take exit 15 and follow Highway 900 south. Turn left on May Valley Rd., and turn left into Squak Mountain State Park. The trailhead is on the left side of the parking lot. The trailhead GPS coordinates are: N47 28.90' / W122 3.26'.

## The Hike

The Issaquah Alps have many outstanding features that rank them among the best recreational assets in the Seattle area, one of those being their proximity to the city. Squak Mountain, the "alp" between Cougar and Tiger Mountains, contains a network of trails crisscrossing the heavily wooded hillsides. The trails can be muddy and some have moderately steep stretches, so trekking poles are a good idea.

Although the Squak Mountain route described in this chapter, which explores the south flank of the mountain, has an approximate 700-foot elevation gain and loss, it was selected to allow hikers to experience the park's natural environment without excessive uphill hiking. The lasso-shaped route begins at the south trailhead at the parking lot and loops clockwise uphill on the lower portion of the Bullitt Creek Trail, up a portion of the South Access Road (closed to motorized public traffic), and down the Equestrian Loop Trail, with a few connector and short-cut trails in between.

A short distance past the trailhead, an optional, flat 0.3-mile interpretive nature trail loops through the forest. To the right of the nature trail, the Bullitt Creek Trail—the beginning of your route—begins.

Squak Mountain's story, like so many in the Pacific Northwest, is one of stewardship and conservation. Until the mid-20th century, Squak Mountain was heavily logged and mined. A prominent Seattle family rescued the mountain from commercial enterprise and donated the land to the state with the proviso that it be allowed to return to its natural state. Today, visitors to Squak Mountain State Park have to look hard to find any reminders of the mountain's commercial past. Nature has reclaimed the mountain with a vengeance. The trails meander up and down through moss- and fern-laden forest, through thickly wooded ravines, and beside and over cascading creeks and waterfalls. You won't find sweeping vistas on this route, but you will find a quiet, meditative forest.

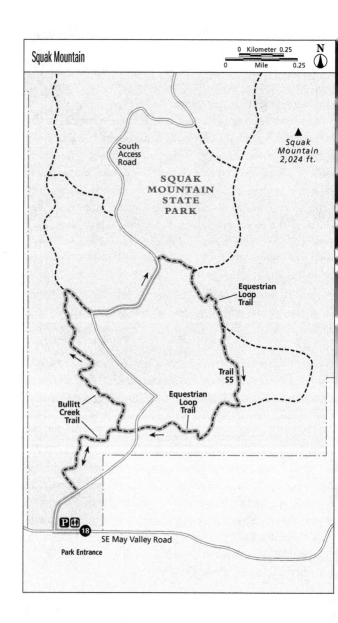

Squak Mountain

0 Kilometer 0.25
0 Mile 0.25

N

Squak
Mountain
2,024 ft.

South
Access
Road

SQUAK
MOUNTAIN
STATE
PARK

Equestrian
Loop
Trail

Trail
S5

Bullitt
Creek
Trail

Equestrian
Loop
Trail

P

18  SE May Valley Road

Park Entrance

Since some Squak Mountain trail junctions are unmarked, it's easy to get lost or inadvertently extend your hike. An excellent supplement to the map provided in this chapter is the trail map available at the trailhead kiosk. With a park map you can follow the route described in this chapter or create your own. If you create your own, be mindful of distance and elevation gain.

## Miles and Directions

**0.0**  The trail begins at the Squak Mountain State park parking lot.

**0.1**  The trail crosses South Access Road and resumes to the right of the nature trail. On the state park trail map, this is identified as the Bullitt Creek Trail.

**0.5**  At a junction, follow the left fork to remain on the Bullitt Creek Trail.

**1.0**  At a junction, follow the right fork, leaving the Bullitt Creek Trail.

**1.2**  The trail joins the South Access Road; turn left and follow the road up the hill.

**1.5**  The Equestrian Loop Trail intersects the road on the right; turn right onto the trail.

**1.6**  At a junction, turn right to remain on the Equestrian Loop Trail and follow it down the hill.

**2.3**  At an easy-to-miss junction, marked as Trail S5, turn right onto S5, a short-cut that leaves and rejoins the main trail. If you miss the junction and remain on the Equestrian Loop Trail, you will simply extend your hike.

**2.5**  Trail S5 ends at the Equestrian Loop Trail; turn right and follow it down the ravine, across the footbridge, and up the hill where it will eventually cross the South Access Road and continue on.

**2.9**  The trail forks; follow the left fork onto the Bullitt Creek Trail.

**3.4**  Arrive back at the trailhead and parking lot.

# 19 Tiger Mountain: Around the Lake Trail

When it comes to a hiking destination, what could be more satisfying than 14,000 acres of heavily forested mountain with 70 miles of hiking trails only thirty minutes from downtown Seattle? That's right . . . nothing. Tiger Mountain serves up a sumptuous spread for the hungry hiker, offering everything from easy nature trails to long, steep terrain. The Around the Lake Trail, which circles Tradition Lake, provides an easy and accessible introduction to Tiger Mountain.

**Distance:** 1.5-mile loop.
**Approximate hiking time:** 1 hour.
**Difficulty:** Easy, flat trail.
**Trail surface:** Dirt.
**Best season:** Year-round, but winter snow and ice conditions can prevent access or make the hike more challenging.
**Other trail users:** None.
**Canine compatibility:** Leashed dogs permitted.

**Fees and permits:** None required.
**Schedule:** Open all year, dawn to dusk. *Caution:* The parking lot gate is locked at dusk.
**Maps:** Any King Co. street map, or USGS Issaquah, WA and Fall City, WA.
**Trail contacts:** State of Washington Department of Natural Resources, (360) 825-1632, www.dnr.wa.gov

**Finding the trailhead:** From Seattle, drive east on Interstate 90 and take exit 20 (High Point). After the exit, turn right, and then take another immediate right onto S.E. 79th St. The trailhead parking lot is at the end of the road. If the gate is closed or the lot is full, park along S.E. 79th St. at the bottom of the hill and walk approximately

.25 mile up to the parking lot. The trailhead GPS coordinates are:
N47 31.78' / W121 59.74'

## The Hike

The third in the series of Issaquah Alps heading east from Seattle is Tiger Mountain. And, like its nearby companions, it was heavily exploited during the Northwest logging boom. A 1910 sawmill and the second longest incline railroad in the US, used to transport the logs down the ridges to the mill, once dominated the mountain.

Although Tiger Mountain is used heavily today for recreation, it is not a park. Instead, Tiger Mountain State Forest is an experimental forest where water and air quality management, wildlife and fish habitat, timber operations, and recreation coexist. The northwest side of Tiger Mountain, the site of the trail route in this chapter, has been designated as the West Tiger Mountain Natural Resources Conservation Area. Logging is prohibited, and preservation of the environment and natural habitat is the top land-management priority, even over recreational use.

Tradition Lake sits on a forested plateau on the other side of a low ridge from Interstate 90, which acts as an effective barrier against traffic noise. The Around the Lake Trail is a short, flat loop that circles the lake a respectable distance from the shore, allowing wildlife undisturbed access to the lake. The trail winds through second-growth forest, lush undergrowth, and some giant Douglas firs that early loggers must have spared. Viewing platforms and benches near the lake, designed to give both humans and wildlife their respective spaces, provide plenty of spots to pause and observe the lake. Signs along the trail identify various animal tracks, a fun feature for kids. The trail joins a power-line access road,

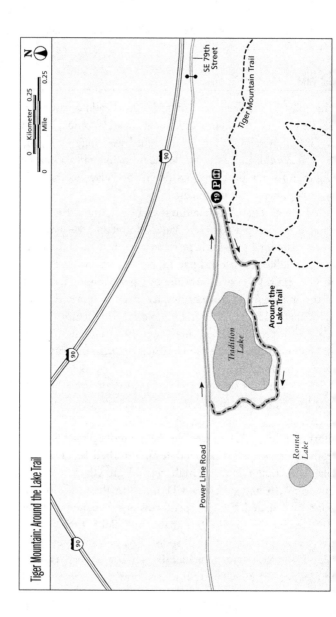

Tiger Mountain: Around the Lake Trail

N

0    Kilometer    0.25

0    Mile    0.25

90

90

90

SE 79th Street

Tiger Mountain Trail

19 P

Around the Lake Trail

Tradition Lake

Power Line Road

Round Lake

losed to public traffic, which follows the north side of the ake and rejoins the trail.

If you have more time for a longer hike, the High Point railhead is the starting point for many trails in the West Tiger Mountain Natural Resources Conservation Area. Be aware of elevation gain and distance before you set out on n alternate hike. Although Tiger Mountain trails tend to be well-signed, a trail map can come in handy.

## Miles and Directions

**0.0** A gated road allows vehicle access to the High Point trailhead parking lot. If the gate is closed, park on the road outside the gate and walk up to the parking lot. The trail begins beside the parking lot near the restrooms. A trail map sign marks the trailhead.

**0.1** At the trail junction, turn right to follow the signed Around the Lake Trail.

**0.5** At the trail junction, turn right to follow the signed Around the Lake Trail.

**0.8** Turn right onto Power Line Road.

**1.4** Turn right onto signed trail to follow Around the Lake Trail back to the trailhead.

**1.5** Arrive back at the trailhead.

# 20 Preston-Snoqualmie Trail: Alice Lake–Snoqualmie Falls Overlook

The historic Preston-Snoqualmie Trail crosses the foothills above the Raging River Valley, a 6.5-mile trail that is a part of the much larger network of King County Regional Trails. This short hike takes in the most scenic portion of the trail, the last few miles at its eastern end. What's so scenic? The trail terminates at a viewpoint that looks across the valley to the 268-foot-high Snoqualmie Falls.

**Distance:** 3.7 miles out-and-back.

**Approximate hiking time:** 1.5–2 hours.

**Difficulty:** Easy, flat trail with one gentle incline.

**Trail surface:** Paved.

**Best season:** Year-round; the winter rainy season adds volume to the falls.

**Other trail users:** Bicyclists, skaters.

**Canine compatibility:** Leashed dogs permitted.

**Fees and permits:** None required.

**Schedule:** Open year-round, dawn to dusk.

**Maps:** Any King Co. street map, or USGS Fall City, WA and USGS Snoqualmie, WA.

**Trail contacts:** King County Parks and Recreation, (206) 296-8687, www.kingcounty.gov/recreation/parks.aspx

**Finding the trailhead:** From Seattle, drive east on Interstate 90 and take exit 22. Turn left, drive over the overpass, turn right at the first intersection, and drive through Preston. The road becomes Preston-Fall City Road S.E. Turn right onto S.E 47th St., right onto Lake Alice Road, and drive up the hill until you reach the well-signed trailhead. Turn right into the parking lot. The trailhead GPS coordinates are: N47 33.05' / W121 53.23'.

## The Hike

Snoqualmie Falls is the site of the region's first hydroelectric plant built in 1898. Still in operation, it provides the Seattle metropolitan area with much of its power.

Nearly 100 feet higher than Niagara Falls, these falls drop from a height of 268 feet, and the width varies based on the time of year and the amount of rainfall. The site of the falls themselves attracts 1.5 million visitors a year, but from the Preston-Snoqualmie Trail, you're likely to have the view of the falls all to yourself.

This paved, straight, gradually graded trail begins in a residential area in rural King County, but soon the residential properties thin out and the trail follows the side of wooded Snoqualmie Ridge high above the Raging River Valley. In spite of the trail's proximity to civilization, a sign at the trailhead with graphics of a bear and cougar remind you that you are treading in wildlife habitat.

The trail follows a historic railroad grade (as do many of the region's trails), which played a major role in populating the fertile valleys at the foot of the Cascades as well as transporting timber and coal. Today, there's no visible evidence of this area's timber and railroad history along this portion of the Preston-Snoqualmie Trail, but history buffs would enjoy a separate visit to the trail's nearby namesake towns: the historic sawmill town of Preston and the railroad town of Snoqualmie, home to the Northwest Railroad Museum with its period depot and impressive collection of vintage railroad cars lining the main street.

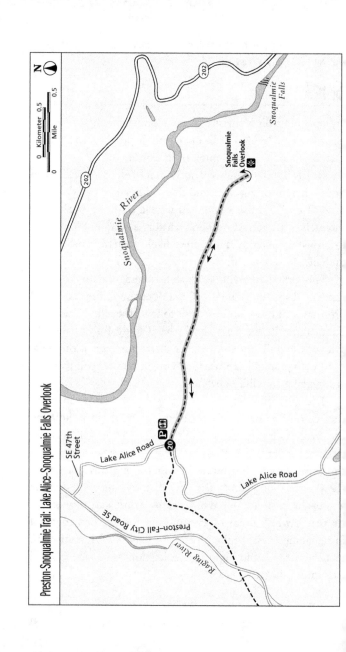

Preston-Snoqualmie Trail: Lake Alice-Snoqualmie Falls Overlook

If walking in a place that had a hand in shaping the region's history holds no interest, the view at the end of the trail surely will: the long drop of Snoqualmie Falls, the visitor center and lodge perched at the top of the falls, and the jagged Cascade peaks rising above it all.

## Miles and Directions

**0.0** The trailhead begins across Lake Alice Road from the parking lot.

**1.8** The trail dead-ends at the Snoqualmie Falls overlook. Turn around and retrace your steps.

**3.7** Arrive back at the trailhead.

# Clubs and Trail Groups

Several environmental, conservation, and hiking resource groups are available in the Seattle area, ranging from clubs where members and participants can enjoy group outings to organizations that are happy to provide information about local trails.

### The Mountaineers
An organization offering trips, classes, and events all related to the Seattle-area outdoors.
7700 Sand Point Way N.E.
Seattle, WA 98115
(206) 521-6000
www.mountaineers.org

### Issaquah Alps Trails Club
A conservation organization offering free guided hikes.
P.O. Box 351
Issaquah, WA 98027
www.issaquahalps.org

### Sierra Club Washington Chapter
Sierra's local chapter offering organized outings and more.
180 Nickerson St., Ste. 202
Seattle, WA 98109
(206) 378-0114
www.sierraclub.org/washington

**Washington Trails Assoc.**
A group providing information about the state's trails.
2019 Third Ave., Ste. 100
Seattle, WA 98121
(206) 625-1367
www.wta.org

# About the Author

Allen Cox, a third generation Northwesterner, enjoys sharing his love of the Pacific Northwest so much that he became chief content officer at *Northwest Travel & Life* magazine. His travel writing has appeared in regional, national, and international publications. He is an honorary lifetime member of International Food, Wine and Travel Writers Association and chair of the Travel & Words Conference. He has a special interest in experiential travel, soft-adventure travel, conservation, and sustainable tourism.

CPSIA information can be obtained
at www.ICGtesting.com
Printed in the USA
BVHW040429160421
605072BV00004B/6

9 781493 053742